THE
TRUTH

Shelley Lubben

TRUTH BEHIND THE FANTASY OF PORN

THE GREATEST ILLUSION ON EARTH

TRUTH BEHIND THE FANTASY OF PORN

For books and other teaching materials please contact:
Shelley Lubben
www.shelleylubben.com

Written by: Shelley Lubben
Cover design: Eric Ridolfi
Interior design: Shelley Lubben
Editor: Mike Valentino

ISBN 13 Digit: 978-1-453-86007-6
Library of Congress information available

Printed in the United States of America

Sources
All scripture quotations, unless otherwise indicated, are taken from the Holy Bible, New International Version®, NIV®. Copyright ©1973, 1978, 1984 by Biblica, Inc.™ Used by permission of Zondervan. Scripture quotations marked NASB are taken from the New American Standard Bible®, Copyright © 1960, 1962, 1963, 1968, 1971, 1972, 1973, 1975, 1977, 1995 by The Lockman Foundation. Used by permission. Scripture quotations marked ESV are taken from The Holy Bible, English Standard Version® (ESV®), copyright © 2001 by Crossway, a publishing ministry of Good News Publishers. Used by permission. Scripture quotations marked NKJV are taken from the New King James Version®. Copyright © 1982 by Thomas Nelson, Inc. Used by permission.

Contents

≈ ACT IV ≈

TWO WORLDS COLLIDE

≈ ACT V ≈

MEET SHELLEY #2

≈ ACT VI ≈

MEET SHELLEY #3

Special Thanks

I would like to express my sincere thankfulness to some of the beautiful people who have helped me since my recovery began in 1995.

To Pastor Kevin Gerald who taught me wisdom and how to live the Champion Life.

To Pat and Argis Hulsey who mentored me in the ways of ministry and taught me: *"Greater is He in you than he that is in the world."*

To Pink Cross Foundation team members who helped me build a beautiful legacy of love and compassion for the hurting.

To Roger my close colleague and a modern day William Wilberforce who is relentless in the cause of human rights.

To Judith Reisman who greatly inspired me by her boldness and unyielding determination to expose the sexual sabotage of our nation.

To Tiffany, Teresa and Abigail who are trophies of God's Grace and sweet angels sent from above to bring healing and beauty into my life.

To Melanie, my best dearest friend and personal servant who ministers to me without fail in great love and humility.

To my beloved and truest friend, my husband Garrett, who rescued me out of the miry pit and led me into vast greatness. I love you Garrett with a fierce and passionate love.

Dedication

I would like to dedicate this book to the hundreds of women and men who died in the porn industry from AIDS, suicide, homicide and drug related deaths.

Your voices will be heard now.

A Word from Shelley

Anyone who would attempt to write a book about their horrific experience inside the illegally operating porn industry and years of sexual abuse from childhood to prostitution faces an awful task, and requires great love and understanding from the readers. This is the hardest thing I've ever had to do and it took years of pain, preparation and prayer before I could do it. But by the grace of God Almighty, I wrote it and now I need you to read it. I need you to read about the exploitation and violence against women and men in the porn industry so you can begin to heal. I need you to earnestly understand that every time you click to view a porn site you are contributing to the destruction of valuable human lives. I need you to read this book through the very last word and then humbly lower your head before heaven and lament in tears until the only strength you have left is to stop viewing pornography.

This book was especially written for my precious friends still trapped inside the porn industry. I humbly request that you read this book and allow me to become your mirror of truth. My heart hurts deeply at the thought of the pain you will encounter as you turn the pages in this book and grasp the evil you are truly enslaved to. But I am confident that once you know the truth, the truth will set you free to throw off the shackles of shame and abuse and victoriously leap into the greatest life you've ever lived!

God bless you all and be free!

★ Admit One ★

★  ★

★ Truth Behind Porn ★

I

★ *Admit One* ★

★ **UNDER THE BIG TOP** ★

★ *Chapter One* ★

You shall know the truth and the truth shall set you free.
- John 8:32

Sex-packed porn films featuring hot dirty blondes whose man-eating eyes say, *"I want you,"* are the greatest illusion on earth. Trust me, I know. I hustled for eight years in strip clubs and whorehouses, manhandling my way to the Big Top, where I was promised fame, fortune and glamour. I was 24 years old when I entered the world of porn.

1

I put on a good show but I never liked performing tricks in the sex circus and preferred spending time with Jack Daniels rather than the male performers I was paid to fake it with. That's right, none of us hot blondes enjoy making porn. In fact, we hate it. We hate spreading our legs for sexually diseased men. We hate being degraded with their foul smells and sweaty bodies. Some women hate it so much that I would hear them vomiting in the bathroom between scenes. I would find others outside, smoking endless chains of Marlboro Lights…

But the multi-billion dollar porn industry wants you to believe the fantasy that we porn actresses love sex. They want you to buy into the lie that we enjoy being degraded by all kinds of repulsive acts. Creatively edited films and prettified packaging are designed to brainwash consumers into believing that the lust we portray on hot and bothered faces are part of the act. But the reality is women are in unspeakable pain from being slapped, bit, spit upon, kicked and called names like "filthy little whore" and "toilet cunt."

While filming the movie "Rough Sex 2," porn star Regan Starr described in horrific terms in an interview with Talk Magazine in February, 2001, "that while sex acts were performed on her, she was hit and choked until she couldn't breathe. Other "actresses," she said, "wept because they were hurting so badly."[1]

Former porn star Jersey Jaxin also described the torment and abuse she experienced on the porn set. "Guys punching you in the face. You have semen all over your face, in your eyes. You get ripped. Your insides can come out of you. It's never ending. You're viewed as an object not as a human with a spirit. People don't care. People do drugs because they can't deal with the way they're being treated."[2]

There is a reason why drugs and alcohol are rampant in the porn industry. Becca Brat, who performed in over 200 movies, told me when she left porn in 2006, "I hung out with a lot of people in the adult industry, everybody from contract girls to gonzo actresses. Everybody had the same problems. Everybody is on drugs. It's an empty lifestyle trying to fill up a void."[3]

Male porn star Christian XXX also speaks openly about the widespread drug use. He wrote on his blog in January, 2008, "I have seen all manner of drugs on set, at parties, in cars, everywhere. If I had to guess, I would put marijuana use at 90 percent of all people involved in the industry (performers, directors, crew, agents, drivers, owners, office workers, etc.). I have been on a set where a girl has passed out DURING a sex scene with me (she was abusing oxycontin). Just recently a girl overdosed on GHB (a party drug that is a clear, odorless drug that doesn't mix well with alcohol) on set. I have seen a girl win a prestigious AVN Award, not show up to accept the award, and then fall into the throes of drug use that caused her to lose at least 50 pounds and drop off the face of the earth."[4]

In fact, porn can literally kill you. Since 2000, there have been at least 34 drug-related deaths among performers.[5]

Offered drinks like vodka and Percocet smoothies, women are numbed enough to endure rough sex acts through extreme humiliation. When alcohol isn't enough and the pain spirals into addiction, porn stars are sent to local doctors in conspiracy with the porn industry to receive prescriptions for Vicodin, Xanax, Valium and other anti-anxiety drugs to help them cope with the trauma.

Former porn actress, Michelle Avanti remembers her first scene and how it led to prescription drug abuse. "I tried backing out and not do porn at all but a male performer said I couldn't back out because I signed a contract. I was threatened that if I did not do the scene I would get sued for lots of money. I ended up taking shots of vodka to get me through it. As I did more and more scenes I abused prescription pills which were given to me anytime by several doctors in the San Fernando Valley. I was given Vicodin, Xanax, Norcos, Prozac and Zoloft. All I had to do was tell them what I needed and they would give me anything I want."[6]

Think I'm exaggerating about the shady operations of the porn industry? Think again. Thanks to the Internet and shows like ABC's 20/20, confessions of rape, drug abuse and violence are increasingly becoming more public. Porn star, Belladonna who told Diane Sawyer, "I always hated porn," confessed how she went to a shoot, preparing for what she thought was a regular sex scene. Instead, the director asked her to do anal sex. According to the network she had just turned 18.

A few months (and several shoots) later, now a veteran porn actress, Belladonna showed up on another set. She was told that she would appear in a prison gang-rape scene, to be shared between twelve different men. Again, she tried to back out. Again, she was "convinced" to continue.[7]

But, you ask, don't women make the choice to be in porn? Based on the sexual images we were spoon fed growing up from TV, magazines and the Internet, sure we do. Beginning in the 1970s when we learned skirt-chasing ways from our favorite stars like Doc in *The Love Boat* all the way to ABC's *Desperate Housewives*, being the most popular show among children in 2005.[8] Not to mention, "glamorous" images of porn stuffed down our throats. It's hardly surprising America's children, most having been well groomed in sexual immorality over 40 years, have ended up on MySpace or Facebook uploading sexy pictures of ourselves. Where else can a hyper sexualized kid get so much attention?

But crooked pornographers have been lurking online for years searching out profiles and preying on unsuspecting sexualized females. Pretending to be teenage boys or male admirers posting flattering words like, "you're the most beautiful girl" or "you're so hot," emotionally needy sexually aware teenage girls quickly fall into their trap. A few compliments later and a nice sized financial offer, we find ourselves standing in the middle of a porn agent's office being talked out of "nude modeling" and into anal sex. "You'll be the next hottest porn star if you do anal," the porn agent promises as we're handed a contract while a big chested blonde in the corner winks at us.

Within days we're sent to the adult industry medical clinic to get tested for sexually transmitted diseases. With open arms and warm smiles, we're welcomed by caring medical staff with calm assurances that we'll be "kept safe." [9] As we begin to feel better about everything we listen carefully to other porn stars who share their tips on how to make it big in porn land. "Just relax your throat and breathe through your nose. It's really fun and easy once you get the hang of it." There is never any proper education about STD's other than a Porn 101 video, which they know none of us would ever watch. Deception is rife throughout the entire grooming process.

Some of us caught HIV as a result of that gross deception.[10] Porn star, Darren James recalls his nightmare of testing positive for HIV in 2004, "It was like a hit in the gut," James said. "Life was pretty much over."[11]

Dr. Sharon Mitchell, "doctor" to the porn stars who walks around in a white lab coat and doesn't have a medical degree, claims that among performers there is, "Less than 7% HIV, and 12-28% STDs. Herpes is always about 66%. Chlamydia and gonorrhea, however, along with hepatitis, seem to stick to everything from dildos to flat surfaces to hands, so, pardon my expression, but we are usually up to our asses in Chlamydia."[12]

But the porn industry is up to its ass in a lot more than that according to the Los Angeles Department of Public Health. In September, 2009, LADPH published astounding reports of 2,396 cases of Chlamydia, 1,389 cases of gonorrhea, and five syphilis cases among porn performers. Between 2004 and 2008, repeat infections were reported for 25.5% of individuals. It was also reported that Chlamydia and gonorrhea prevalence in porn performers is *ten times higher* than that of Los Angeles County 20-24 year olds and *five times higher* that of one of Los Angeles County's highest risk populations. To top that off, 25 cases of HIV were reported by the Adult Industry Medical Healthcare Foundation (AIM) since 2004. AIM is the adult industry medical clinic that offers testing services and *limited* medical care to porn stars. Due to the failure of talent testing clinics to routinely screen for rectal and oral infections, a sustained high level of prevalent disease persists among porn performers.[13]

In addition to being coerced, lied to and repeatedly exposed to non-curable life-threatening diseases, many women experience severe damage to internal body parts. Former porn star Kami Andrews confesses she loves the money and the glamour of porn but what she doesn't like is not being able to "s--- right. You are constantly doing enemas and you're fasting and you're taking all these different pills, ex lax, and it screws up your internal system."[14]

Screwed up intestinal tracts is only the beginning of extreme bodily damage caused by hardcore anal acts. Many women experience other medical maladies such as a prolapsed rectum, a horrific condition in which the walls of the rectum protrude through the anus and consequently become visible outside the body. Eventually the damage becomes permanent -- to the twisted delight of beastly pornographers who have crafted a way to turn this unspeakable condition into a "fetish."

When porn stars call it a day and head home with bruised and bloodied bodies, some of us attempt to have normal healthy relationships but our suitcase pimp boyfriends become jealous and physically abuse us. So instead we marry our porn directors or regress back to childhood and freeload off of 60 year old sugar daddies. I preferred sugar daddies because I desperately wanted the love and attention of my father. Jenna Jameson, Jill Kelly, Rita Faltoyano, and Tera Patrick preferred marrying within the porn industry and are all now victims of what Porn star Tera Patrick calls "the porn curse." She states in her book about divorce, "I didn't want to be another porn statistic."[15]

Porn stars not only don't make good wives but we miserably fail as mothers too. We yell and scream and hit our kids for no reason. Most of the time we are intoxicated or high, and our four year olds are the ones picking our lifeless bodies up off the floor. When big dollar clients come over to be entertained by our tricks, we lock our children in their bedrooms and tell them to be quiet. I used to give my four-year old daughter a beeper and make her wait at the park until I was finished. For those of us who are married, Daddy doesn't mind babysitting the kids while we're at work being penetrated by several male performers. Of course not, our narcissistic porn husbands only care about the money.

The truth is there *is no* fantasy in porn. It's *all* an illusion. A closer look into the hardcore scenes of a porn star's life will show you an act the porn industry doesn't want you to see. The real truth is we porn actresses want to end the shame and trauma of our box office lives but we can't do it alone. We need you men to fight for our freedom and give us back our honor. We need you to hold us in your strong arms while we sob tears over our deep wounds and begin to heal. We want you to throw out our movies and help piece together the shattered fragments of our lives. We need you to pray for us so God will hear and repair our ruined lives.

Don't believe the big top fantasy. Porn is nothing more than fake sex, bruises and lies on video. Trust me, I know.

★ SEND IN THE CLOWNS ★

★ *Chapter Two* ★

My porn name was Roxy and I performed my circus tricks in about 30 hardcore movies between 1993 and 1994. From anals to facials to gangbangs and interracials, there was nothing I wouldn't do to prove to the world that I would become the next hottest porn star sensation. I could juggle and ball-spin with the best of them.

I began my porn training at nine years old when I was sexually abused by a female classmate and her teenage brother in a swimming pool. I was a normal kid who did culturally normal things like play with Barbie dolls and watch Sesame Street when out of the blue my Ken doll decided to take the fantasy too far and pull down his trunks and violate Barbie in the deep end. I became a damaged "dirty" little girl overnight.

Damaged little girls are exactly what the porn industry preys upon and depends upon. It is estimated that 90% of porn performers are sexual abuse survivors and the average age of a porn actress is 22.8 years old.[16] [17] I repeat, *damaged little girls*. According to former porn actress April Garris, counselor to ex porn stars, "in most every single case, there is some background of childhood sexual abuse or neglect."[18]

Porn queen Jenna Jameson, who is the most downloaded porn star on the Internet, was also a damaged little girl before entering porn. In Jameson's autobiography she describes the painful neglect and drug use of her father, two teenage rapes, drug addictions, and numerous affairs with men and women. Jenna claims her rapes had nothing to do with her choice for a porn career.[19] She has what I like to term the *classic porn star background*.

The classic porn star background (CPSB) is a realistic compilation of a porn star's past and current traumatic experiences which include childhood sexual abuse, exposure to pornographic material, parental neglect, physical abuse, verbal abuse, family dysfunction, substance abuse, rape, and sexual revictimization. The cumulative effect of all of these negative experiences causes victims to unconsciously develop powerful self-protection systems known as defense mechanisms.

DEFENSE MECHANISM

Definition:

Self-protection system designed to lessen or repress certain thoughts, feelings or memories from entering the conscious mind.

TOP 10 PORN STAR DEFENSE MECHANISMS

(1) **Acting out** - performing an extreme behavior in order to express thoughts or feelings the person feels incapable of otherwise expressing.

(2) **Denial** - refusing to acknowledge some painful aspect of external reality or subjective experience that would be apparent to others.

(3) **Displacement** - taking out frustrations, feelings and impulses on people or objects that are less threatening. For example, violence against women by pornographers who feel anger toward their mothers.

(4) **Fantasy** - using daydreaming or imagination to escape from reality into a fictitious world of success or pleasure.

(5) **Humor** - pointing out the funny or ironic aspects of a situation in order to deal with it. For example, making jokes about one's sexually transmitted diseases.

(6) **Idealization** - attributing exaggerated positive qualities to others such as thinking highly of a "friendly" pornographer.

(7) **Omnipotence** - feeling or acting as if he or she possesses special powers or abilities and is superior to others.

(8) **Projection** - denying one's own unpleasant traits, behaviors, or feelings by attributing them to someone else. For example, accusing Shelley Lubben of being an attention whore.

(9) **Rationalization** - explaining an unacceptable behavior or feeling in a rational or logical manner, avoiding the true reasons for the behavior. For example, a porn star who is turned down for a job might rationalize by saying the producer prefers to shoot ugly girls anyways.

(10) **Repression** - The unconscious exclusion of painful impulses, desires, or fears from the conscious mind. Often involving sexual or aggressive urges or painful childhood memories, these unwanted mental contents are pushed into the unconscious mind.

In carny terms, porn stars are trained seals and hard acts to follow. We are trapeze artists, magicians, clowns, acrobats, contortionists and tight-rope walkers. We are the world's greatest performers and practiced liars. When we were sexually abused as children we were forced to believe that we were good for only one thing. Sex. We were afraid to tell so we never had a choice to appeal or to heal from our sexual wounds and neglect, so we felt discarded and turned into angry revengeful little girls acting out our pain to get attention.

But our parents wouldn't pay attention. Churches wouldn't pay attention nor did our schools pay any attention. In fact, nobody paid attention to the freaks of nature we had morphed into. Surely our deformities were noticeable. We were bed wetters, sexual deviants, peculiar rebels who plucked out their eyelashes and played with their genitals. We were molesters of other children and even scolded for it. Our childhood games consisted of hide and seek my private parts and truth and dare you to show me yours and I'll show you mine. Our freak show was on center stage for our parents and the entire world to see. But *nobody* paid attention. Nobody ever asked us what happened and we were left to ourselves in tears and shame to survive and train for the only thing we believed we were good for: filthy dirty sex.

As we entered our teenage years we discovered that our sexuality could be used as a tool to gain back control and get even with society for ignoring us for so long. We followed older rebellious role models like Madonna and expressed ourselves in skimpy skirts and tight little shirts. It made perfect sense to us, since we knew that we'd gain the same sick admiration from boys and older males that she received from the world. We manipulated our classmates with sensual conduct and sexual favors and grew in superior knowledge of the great power we possessed.

When we entered our adult years we became sexual spectacles and demanded higher payment in the form of attention *and* cash as compensation for the neglect and sexual abuse that we suffered as children. I like to call it porn star currency. We will lie to get it. We will steal to get it. We will prostitute ourselves and risk our lives to get it. Porn stars can juggle HIV, Gonorrhea and Chlamydia while we fearlessly reinfect ourselves with even more STD's. We can do amazing feats with our minds and bodies that would terrify most ordinary people. We can walk a thin line of death and life at great heights without any fear of falling. With the help of drugs and alcohol our skills are enhanced to tolerate huge amounts of physical, mental and emotional pain. Our infected bodies are covered with sores and traces of bruises hidden beneath our daring and flaring images. We are pornographic superstars performing in the world's greatest freak show at a website near you!

Heroic as the "supers" may appear many porn stars have tragically and sadly plunged into their untimely deaths. Out of about 1,500 performers between 2007 and 2010, 34 people *that we know of* died from AIDS, suicide, drugs and homicide. 17 more performers died prematurely from medical causes to include lung disease, heart failure and cancer.[20, 21] That is a total of 51 premature deaths. No other industry has these kinds of statistics, not even the music industry which is at least 10 times bigger than the porn industry.

In 2009, the music industry released 97,751 albums compared to only 13,056 (including amateur) total porn titles released.[22, 23] Between 2007 and 2009 there were 9 drug related deaths and 2 suicides among singers and musicians in an industry of 12,765 recording companies compared to 10 drug related deaths and 8 suicides in an industry of only about 900 porn companies.[24, 25, 26, 27] That is one death for every 1,160 recording companies versus one death for every 50 porn companies. It doesn't take a math genius to understand that the porn industry is drastically smaller than the music industry and yet has higher rates of drug-related deaths and suicides. I repeat, *no other industry destroys more people than the porn industry!*

Furthermore, when the deaths of 129 porn stars over a period of roughly 20 years were analyzed it was discovered that the average life expectancy of a porn star is only 37.43 years whereas the average life expectancy of an American is 78.1 years.[28]

As recently as June, 2010, male porn star Stephen Hill killed a coworker and injured two others in a sword attack at a porn studio in Van Nuys, California. The victim was 30-year-old male porn actor Herbert Wong. The sad and tragic events don't end there. A police manhunt ensued and Stephen was tracked down at his Chatsworth home. The 34-year-old porn star died after falling from a cliff after a standoff with the Los Angeles Police Department SWAT team. He was heard to have said shortly before his death, "It wasn't supposed to happen this way."

The porn industry was never supposed to happen this way. But 1 out of 4 Americans made it happen. While women and men in porn destroyed themselves with drugs, alcohol and suicide we sat idly by at our computers with "popcorn" in one hand and our mouse in the other greedily clicking away at their lives. May God forgive our evil.

Sad and painted face
who makes the masses roar
Lions, seals and trapeze thrills
while you, the sad faced whore
There must be something more
than death and circus gore
What are you dying for?
by Shelley Lubben

15

★ *Admit One* ★

★  ★

★ *Meet Shelley #1* ★

★ *Admit One* ★

★ BORN TO BE BAD ★

★ *Chapter Three* ★

Born Shelley Lynn Moore on May 18, 1968 in Pasadena, California, I come from a long line of Methodist preachers on my mother's side and Catholic Italians on my father's side. My father and mother were opposites in nature and upbringing but very much in love and my sister and brother were born a couple of years after me. I am the eldest and only brunette child with green eyes a.k.a. the WOP. My mother called me her WOP (without papers) because I looked like a little grape-smasher.

I grew up in a middle class home in Temple City, California, where my family regularly attended a good church in Alhambra. That's where I met the love of my life, Jesus. Every Sunday my teacher told me marvelous stories about Jesus and how He had compassion and healed thousands of sick people. Oh how I loved Jesus! My favorite part of the class was when my Sunday School teacher took out her brown ukulele and played the most beautiful music. With my head titled back and my eyes tightly shut I sang my little heart out to Jesus, "Oh how I love Jesus. Oh how I love Jesuuus." Everything just disappeared. It was Jesus and I in our own special place.

"Oh how I love Je-SUUUS," I bursted again.

But oh how I hated when I saw my parents standing at the door and it was time for Sunday School to end. I just wanted to listen to my Sunday School teacher tell me more Bible stories while I munched on Ritz crackers.

In 1977, our family moved away from my happy Christian life to a small fairly upscale town called Glendora, or as I used to call it, Glenboring. In a town filled with orange groves and a population of about 20,000 people there wasn't much to do except have an orange fight. I was ready for a fight too. I was pretty angry that we had to leave the only friends and family I had ever known and loved. Sunday School and Ritz crackers were my life!

By then my little brother was born and completely attached to my mother's breast. So my sister and I were pretty much left to ourselves playing with our Barbie dolls and watching hours and hours of television. My mother always said television was the best babysitter. Well, with a babysitter like that I learned a lot! As a kid, I learned more about sex from shows like "Three's Company" and "Love American Style" than I did anywhere else. With a weekly lineup of comedies about increased sex drive who needed puberty?

And then there was the spin-off to "Love American Style", a show called "Happy Days," where I really learned the facts of life. With a bag of Fritos in my lap and my face glued to the TV set I got to watch Fonzie make out with chicks at Inspiration

Point. Could TV get any hotter than this for a nine-year-old? Or how about when our family gathered around to watch "All in the Family", a show that had to have a disclaimer the first time it aired. Thanks to Archie Bunker my family listened to racial slurs for years. "All In The Family" also taught me about politics, swingers, women's rights, and homosexuality. Oh yeah, I learned a lot from television.

Television wasn't my only teacher. I also learned a lot from the teenage boy and his sister who sexually molested me when I was nine years old. It conveniently happened in my friend's swimming pool when no parents were around. There we were all alone - me, my friend and her *very* cute older brother.

How I was talked into skinny dipping by my new friend I don't have a clue but I remember thinking that if I didn't do it, the whole school was going to find out and call me a chicken. I reluctantly peeled off my bathing suit and quickly stepped into the pool to cover up my naked body. The only memories I have after that is of her teenage brother walking over to the edge of the pool where his sister and I were swimming and he started teasing us. His sister splashed water back at him and told him to go away but he just laughed and pulled his pants down and jumped in. I ripped my head away in embarrassment and swam rapidly to the other side of the pool in hopes my bathing suit was nearby. When I looked back to see where they were I saw both of them underwater and heading straight for me.

The next thing I felt was indescribable. I saw her brother's golden head beneath the water coming toward me near the surface. When his head came up for air our eyes met and I just stared into his handsome face with awe. No older boy had ever been this close to me. I could feel his warm breath on my face while I stood there frozen staring into his big blue eyes. He reached his hand over and started touching me between my legs. A strange tingly feeling took over my whole body and I couldn't move or breathe.

A hard poke against my stomach brought me back to reality and I thought it must have been his thumb.

"That feels really big," I remember thinking. I looked down and saw his "thing" and my mouth fell open. That's when I blanked out.

Fear abruptly woke me up out of my shock and thoughts of getting into trouble raced through my mind.

What will my mother do if she finds out? Did anybody see us? What if the kids at school find out?

A sick feeling washed over me.

I shoved him away with all of my might and swam as fast as I could to the other end of the pool where my bathing suit was. Pulling myself up out of the water over the edge, I grabbed my suit and frantically put it back on while searching for the nearest towel.

"Towel, towel, where's a towel?" I asked myself as I anxiously looked around. I spotted a blue towel and threw it around my shoulders and ran out of the gate into the house at full throttle.

I locked myself in the bathroom while I listened to my friend yell and pound on the door for about thirty minutes.

"Come out of there, Shelley! My brother didn't really mean it."

Yeah, right.

Wiping the tears away I finally worked up enough nerve to come out of the bathroom. I slipped into her bedroom where the guest bed was and covered myself up to my neck with the bed sheets. Nobody was going to put their hands on me again. I tried to keep my eyes open all night but I was so traumatized that I fell asleep almost right away.

Awakened by a dark shadowy figure hovering over me I gasped, "What is that???"

I opened my eyes to find long blonde hair dangling in my face. It was too dark to see much but I felt something weird rubbing against my thighs. My eyes adjusted to the darkness and shockingly I saw my friend on top of me moving her hips around while making moaning sounds. I forcefully pushed my friend off of me and curled up on the edge of the bed into a sobbing ball. I just wanted to go home.

The rest of the night I laid there in shock, staring into the still darkness while creepy voices whispered into my head, "You're a bad dirty girl."

I was too young to understand all that had transpired that day, but the dirty and shameful seeds that were planted deep within my being that night would continue to grow over the next seventeen years of my life. Watered by neglect and verbal abuse the small satanic seeds that were embedded in my soul would gradually mature into an adult world of fully-grown fruits of wickedness.

And then I could be *really* bad.

★ *Admit One* ★

★ RAISING HELL ★

★ *Chapter Four* ★

I swore up and down to the cop I only drank one beer but he still made me get out of my car and walk the stupid line. I slapped my hand down on the dashboard and kicked my car door open with my six inch red stilettos. That pig definitely picked the wrong girl to mess with. Not only could I walk the line under the influence of a fifth of Jack Daniels but I could re-cite the entire alphabet backwards faster than any human being alive.

"ZYXWVUTSRQPONMLKJIHGFEDCBA."

The cop just stood there with his jaw dropped. Then he smiled and offered to take me out for a drink. It was just another day in the sex biz for me.

Was I always this bad, you ask? Of course I wasn't. Okay, okay, I admit I was pretty bad but I didn't start off like that. I was a barely decent kid until I was about 14 years old and *then* I discovered boys. I discovered that if I let a boy feel my boobies he would tell me, "I love you." Oh how I longed to hear those words from my father.

My mom on the other hand loved to communicate and call me names like, "lazy", "forgetful", "hyper" and "weird". She also used to nag and belittle me to death. If there's anything I remember about being a teenager it was the daily constant fighting between her and me. My mother verbally and emotionally bulldozed me much of my junior high and high school years.

I think the hate affair between my mother and I began when I was five years old and my brother was about to be born. I was a jealous little girl who *desperately* craved attention because I wasn't getting enough of it. In a last bid attempt to make my parents notice me before my brother arrived, I began making up wild stories about men who tried to kidnap me. When my parents became upset and showed signs of concern for me, I felt like someone had given me a breath of fresh air. But eventually I caved in and told them the truth. I wasn't an experienced practiced liar *yet*.

My sister in stark contrast was a perfect angel. Two years younger than me with the disposition and coloring of a golden cocker spaniel, my mother loved her. Of course, she loved her. She was the easy kid.

However, I was the mad scientist in the family. Gifted with ESP, extra special personality, I had that little thing called "it." "It" was something that everybody else didn't have that I did have. As my mother liked to label it, I was *peculiar*.

Born into this world with boundless amounts of energy, I was a talking, walking, dancing, writing, acting and shocking machine. A rising star with humble beginnings in my backyard, I wrote, directed and starred in my first play at six years old. When my first grade teacher told my mother that I amazed her, I was emotionally swept off of my feet. To my mother I was a peculiar pain in the ass but to my affectionate teacher, I was William Shakespeare.

The first time I ever performed on a real stage I was eight years old. After a successful audition where I huffed and I puffed and blew my teacher's notes down, I was given the lead part as the Big Bad Wolf in a school play. The other kids just stood there with their mouths dropped. While they clumsily read lines off of their papers, mine were memorized. I marched on that stage and puffed out my words with such a ferocious growl that I almost blew the roof off the cafeteria. Hands down, I got the part.

It was obvious I was made for the stage, but the gift in me was never developed as it should have been. My young mother was embarrassed by her eccentric daughter and didn't know what to do with me. My father, who labeled himself as "the mechanical man", was too busy living his machine-like life to pay much attention to his creative daughter. A man with a genius IQ and an electrical wizard, my father was himself a creative mad scientist. Whenever I wanted to talk with him during the day, all I had to do was go out to the garage or look under the car to find him. If I wanted to talk to him at night, I could find him reclining in his favorite chair in front of the TV. It was TV, the garage or the hardware store. I loved when my Dad spent time with me and took me to the hardware store. I can still smell the colorful wires hanging from the wall.

My mother was my father's complete opposite. She *really* confused me. Born into the family of a Pentecostal Preacher, my mother was the last of five children. She was the "accident" child. Raised in a strict religious home, the worst thing she ever did was sneak a listen to an Elvis song. How my father, the Catholic-raised mechanical wizard and electric guitar player, ever connected with my mother, Your Holiness, remains a mystery to me. But they were very much in love and in fact my mother used to tell me, "Your father I can't replace. But you we can make more of." She was a talkative woman whose cold words were like knives thrust into my heart.

While my mother venomously preached religion to me, she rarely demonstrated the love and truth of Jesus Christ to me. I or someone else was always going to hell for something. My mother was the ultimate judge of humanity and prejudiced against people of other ethnic backgrounds or status. I never understood her actions because my grandfather, her father, was such a sensitive and loving man. When we did go on a rare visit to my grandparents, I could always count on my grandfather to take me on long walks on the beach where he described to me in tears the awesome love of Christ. In his later years, when I asked him to give me his very best piece of advice, he whispered, "Shelley, you must practice the Presence of God." A few months later he died at ninety-eight years old.

Confused by Christianity and glued to the TV, I became a daydreamer and imagined what it would be like to be famous. More than anything I wanted to be like the actors I saw on TV who were adored and cherished by millions of people. *I wanted* to be adored and loved by millions of people. *I wanted* to receive the long applauses and standing ovations. When I finally unglued myself from hours of television and daydreaming, I expressed myself through poetry or short stories and plays. I wrote my first poem called, "Nature" when I was eight years old. I wrote my first book at nine years old and even designed the book cover. It was the only book written by a child accepted into the school library. I also learned how to play guitar and even tried the violin for a while but with little encouragement, I never developed my musical gifting.

I was the world's greatest starter and worst finisher. With no one to regularly encourage me and teach me discipline, I was left to myself where I devised mischievous ways to express my creativity and gain what I desired most: *attention.*

When I was about nine years old I began acting out and gave myself the nickname "Shellshock". Living up to my name and out of pure boredom, I created a list of shocking things to do and convinced some of my friends to join me. One day we were going down the list and it read, "Pretend to be dead." We nodded. I immediately ran inside the house and got a bottle of ketchup and squirted it all over my arms and face. I handed the ketchup to my friend Stella who kept an eye out behind the bush while I lay down in the street next to the curb with my glasses hanging out of my hand. It was pure genius. Moving cars came to a halted screech and concerned mothers ran over to see why a bleeding girl was lying in the street. When they bent down to see if I was breathing, I popped up and said, "Just kidding!" and took off running.

Another time when I was bored and wanted attention, I found a small piece of black cloth that looked like a spider. I knew my mother was fiercely afraid of spiders, especially Black Widows, so I wanted to scare her to death. I took my tiny spider looking cloth and threw it at my mother and screamed, "Spider!" I never saw my mother jump so high in my life. She was so mad with me. Of course, I ran.

My favorite place to run to was the little Baptist Church on the corner. They knew I was a little villainess and they loved me anyway. The one person who especially loved me was Mrs. Mumby. She was the little gray haired teacher who put up with me every summer in Vacation Bible School. One day while Mrs. Mumby was getting something out of the supply closet, I shoved her in and locked it. As I was laughing hysterically while pointing at the closet, she pounded and screamed, "Let me out, Shelley! Let me out!" I laughed even harder. The other kids looked at me like I was Satan. When nobody had the key to open the closet and the Fire Department came to rescue her, it wasn't so funny anymore. Mrs. Mumby stepped out ready to faint from heat exhaustion. I felt really bad about that one.

But then again I felt bad about everything happening in my life. I was a dirty, lonely, shocking little girl on a desperate hunt for love and attention. The only person who truly understood me was my Italian grandmother, Nonnie. Now *she* was magical.

"Cigarette me, baby, and light me up," she'd say in a sexy voice as she tilted her head back and pretended to dangle her long cigarette holder. My Nonnie loved to impersonate Mae West, Hollywood's first superstar sex symbol and original blonde bombshell who was arrested in 1918 for "corrupting morals of youth."

Well, maybe my Nonnie corrupted me a little.

She was a captivating woman and eloquent speaker who had the powerful ability to influence anyone in her presence. A petite olive-skinned woman with beautiful jet black hair pinned up, she was the most glamorous woman I had ever seen.

Every December my glamorous grandmother would visit us for the holidays and stay with our family through mid January. It was the best six weeks out of my unfulfilled life. For six weeks I had someone in my life who consistently told me, "I love you". For six weeks there was someone who cared enough *to take the time* to teach me things like the importance of washing my hands before a meal. For six weeks I learned how to fold fancy napkins, set a proper dinner table and how to make Veal Scaloppini. For six weeks I received the love, gentle instruction and encouragement I needed to be successful in life. And for six whole weeks I actually felt good about myself because of the sense of accomplishment I had gained. And then Nonnie would leave and I would fall back into my lazy and rebellious ways until she came back the following year.

Unfortunately, by the time I was a teenager I was too full of anger and frustration to try and be an angel every Christmas. Quite the opposite, I had become the teenager from hell. With role models like Madonna to encourage me and parents who hid their heads in the sand, I was allowed to do *whatever* I wanted. I was allowed to go to a senior prom in a limousine with an older non-Christian boy where I got drunk for the first time. My Dad had to drive all the way to Los Angeles to pick me up in a prom dress with holes all over it. Apparently I was so drunk I burned holes through my dress with a clove cigarette. It was the polk-a-dotted purple prom dress from hell.

At 14 years old, I was allowed to wear a Playboy bunny costume for Halloween with bunny ears, garter belt, fluffy tail and all. My mother took the picture. I was also given permission to drive my mother's Thunderbird to nightclubs at age 16 and *then* I was allowed to drive around my 15 year old boyfriend with whom I was having sex. Yes, we had sex in my mother's car. When she asked me the next day what the spot on her seat was I coolly replied, "Vanilla shake."

I was also allowed to have a birthday party in my house where we drank alcohol while my parents watched television in their bedroom. Okay, so they didn't know we brought in alcohol but what parents allow their rebellious sixteen year old daughter to have a party without parental supervision? I even got my 13 old sister to drink.

For most of my teenage life I was pretty much allowed to do *whatever* I wanted because nobody cared.

Nobody cared if I had a drinking problem at age 16. Nobody cared if I was flunking classes or receiving bad grades. Nobody cared if I wore fishnet stockings to school. Nobody cared if I was having underage sex. Nobody cared if I was a reckless driver and got my driver's license suspended. Nobody cared if I went to jail for stealing from Target. Nobody cared about anything I did.

When my father decided to *care* about his family and put his foot down and take a firm stand, he threw open the front door and told me to "Get out!" followed by four heartless words that I have never forgotten.

"You're dead to me."

In shock, I furiously walked out the door with a bag of clothes and a Bible swearing to God I would never talk to my father or mother again for as long as I lived. Over again those words repeated in my head, "You're dead to me."

"You're dead to me." Rejection entered in.

"You're dead to me." Hate entered in.

"You're dead to me." Rage entered in.

And Satan entered into my heart and then all hell broke loose on the next eight years of my life.

★ *Admit One* ★

★ HELL OF A HOOKER ★

★ *Chapter Five* ★

A brazen blonde bomb-*shell* with stage names like "Marilyn" and "Blondie", I hustled myself through eight years of stripping, prostitution and plenty of porn. I started my career at a strip club called "The Top Hat" at seventeen years old when I still lived at home in Glendora, California. It wasn't hard to steal an older girl's I.D. and dupe the owner into it and besides I could dance. I could dance so well that even Michael Jackson would have been proud. In fact, my first audition, I did the moonwalk topless to "Billie Jean" while men in plaid shirts whistled and threw crumpled dollar bills at me. When I flipped my head around and saw those truckers slide off their stools to come and get a closer look at me, I jumped off the stage and ran straight for the front doors swearing to God I would never strip again.

Never say never.

I ended up a year later on a grimy curb in the San Fernando Valley, the porn capital of the world, where I sat on the edge of a busy street crying my eyes out with sobs flying out of my throat. I hadn't eaten for two days and I was starving. I thought about getting a job but I didn't have a driver's license. I tried begging for money but nobody wanted to help. My situation seemed hopeless. I looked over at the black Bible I brought with me and cried out to Jesus for answers.

"Jesus, where are you!? How could you let this happen to me? You told me when I was a little girl that I would preach the Gospel to thousands of people. Now I'm sitting here homeless with nothing to eat or drink. I need you to do a miracle right now!"

I sat there under the hot sun and sobbed for hours on that faded and cracked curb on Sherman Way. Desperate and dehydrated, I didn't care if I died.

To my surprise I heard a man's voice and I looked up and saw a handsome well-built black man staring down at me. He looked like an angel.

"What's wrong, honey? Why are you crying?" he asked as he sat down next to me on the curb.

With swollen eyes and spit hanging out of my mouth I spluttered, "I'm homeless and I don't have uh any...," sniff sniff, "food or money. My dad kicked me out of the house and I don't know what to do."

I sobbed even harder and lowered my head into my sticky hands to hide my tears. I was so ashamed and humiliated. The nice man put his arms around me and gently pulled me towards him. When my head landed on his chest I felt an inexplicable relief. It was the first time in my life that an older man had held me so tenderly. It felt *so good*. I never wanted to leave that feeling. I just wanted to stay wrapped in his arms and rest my head on his big warm chest.

After he held me for a few minutes he gently turned my chin towards him and said to me, "I can help you, honey. I can get you some money and some food."

Immediately I thought Jesus had come to rescue me. I sat up excitedly to listen closely to the handsome man as he continued. "There's a man in the apartment complex across the street who thinks you're real pretty and would like to make love to you for $35."

"What???" My mouth dropped open. Was this man asking me to be a prostitute? I was a lot of things but I definitely wasn't a prostitute.

"No way!" I said as I sat back in disgust.

But he assured me in a soft-spoken voice that the man who wanted to have sex with me was very nice and would be gentle with me. He told me he could get me a lot of money and that I could get my own apartment and I wouldn't have to live on the street anymore. I began to think about my parents and what they did to me. I thought about how they were sleeping sound-ly in their comfortable beds while I sat here on the curb all day and night with no money or food. I thought about the last cold-hearted words my father said to me, "You're dead to me".

That's when I heard a low voice whisper into my head, "God doesn't care. Your parents don't care..." and full of hatred I thought to myself, *yeah, why should I care?* And I agreed to sell myself for $35.

I was so nervous when he opened the door. The room was dark and I could barely see what the man looked like.

"Hello," an older voice called out as I shut the door behind me.

I didn't answer or make a sound. We were just two com-plete strangers standing in the dark together. He moved closer to me and pulled my head towards his face. I tried to turn away but he held my head tightly and kissed me. After a couple of minutes I began to feel comfortable because the man was very gentle. In fact, I remember thinking he kissed *much better* than the high school boys I had dated.

This isn't so bad after all, I thought to myself.

And I walked away with thirty-five big ones. After the pimp lured me in with a nice first trick, he started to set me up with perverse men who demanded bizarre sex. When I refused to do certain sex acts, the pimp threatened me with physical abuse and tried to lock me in his apartment. But I was so full of rage that I busted out of his big black arms and ended up on another curb on Ventura Boulevard.

By then I was in full survival mode. I started walking the streets boldly asking men if they wanted to have sex for money. One time I approached a mechanic shop and the manager took me into the restroom where he ejaculated and bled all over my face. The blood scared me so badly that I knew I had to get off the streets. I ran out of the mechanic shop in tears crying out to God for help. But there was no answer.

I soon met a girl named Beth who warned me that I was going to get killed if I kept walking the streets. She introduced me to Vanessa, a madam who ran a prostitution house. I really didn't want to do prostitution anymore in any form so I begged Vanessa to let me weed her lawn in exchange for letting me stay a couple of months. She tried to talk me into turning tricks but I was too traumatized after the pimp and the blood so I adamantly said no. She knew what she was doing though. Every morning she gave me a shovel and a trash can and made me work eight hours a day under the hot California sun. While I was dying in the heat and wiping the sweat off of my muddy brow, the other girls were sitting comfortably inside an air-conditioned house wearing lingerie and drinking iced teas. I would watch the men come through the gate one by one and exactly one hour later I watched them walk back out with a huge smile. The girls looked really happy too. They were counting their money while I was shoveling dirt. And that same low voice came to me again and said, "God doesn't care. Your parents don't care…"

Yeah, I thought. *Why should I care what anyone thinks?* So I sold myself again only this time for $150.

Vanessa taught me things my mother never taught me. For starters, she taught me about feminine hygiene. After a client complained about me and I was utterly humiliated, Vanessa threw a sponge at me and taught me how to properly wash and groom myself. She was the most brazen and unashamed woman I'd ever met. Not only did she teach me about cleanliness but she taught me how to manipulate men in a variety of ways. I learned things like how to put a condom on a man without him ever knowing it. I learned how to fake an orgasm for men who wanted to be heroes.

"Oh yeah, baby I'm gonna cum."

Yeah, right.

I learned how to barter sex for clothes, jewelry and furniture. Vanessa and I would regularly visit jewelry shops on Ventura Boulevard and make "deals" with the owners. I was never without rings on my fingers.

I also learned how to talk clients into giving me more money. Vanessa taught me how to stall sex acts and redirect men to talk about their fantasies until their hour was up and then they had to pay me more in order to have the actual sex. I used to brag endlessly that I could clean any man's wallet out. And I was merciless. I wanted every last nickel and penny from those selfish needy pigs that required a prostitute for an hour. How pathetic.

What is more pathetic is that I got pregnant twice during the first fourteen months I was a prostitute. Though I was taught to be careful and use condoms, unfortunately I learned the hard way that condoms can *and will* break or leak. In fact, men often-times tried to break condoms on purpose. That's how piggish they were. I learned a lot of hard lessons that first year of prostitution. I learned that losing a baby was extremely physically and emotionally painful. I was only eight weeks pregnant when I lost my first baby. I blamed myself and swore I would never do prostitution again. So I left Vanessa's house and hitchhiked my way to downtown Los Angeles, where I found a job as a "taxi dancer" in a Hostess Club. Taxi dancing is really just a form of prostitution with clothes on but of course I didn't know that. I thought there were men in this world who actually wanted to dance!

I sat on that couch every night at 8 o'clock waiting for some strange man to punch my time card so I could get paid. Lined up on a red sofa with other young blondes and brunettes, I felt like a piece of candy in a candy store.

"Pick me", I thought as I smiled at each man as he walked through the door. I saw skinny ones, fat ones, and mostly old ones walk through that door each night.

One night an Asian man picked me and led me to a spot on the darkly lit dance floor where nobody else was around. He slipped a hundred-dollar bill into my hand and started rubbing himself against my thigh. I didn't want him to ejaculate on my dress like the last guy had done so I suggested we go to a booth for more privacy. I learned real fast that men wanted hand jobs, not dances.

When we got to the booth I tried to stall him in order to get out of doing a sexual favor. He ended up liking me and offered me two hundred *more* dollars to have dinner with him. Of course I said yes and fell in love with his money right away. He told me his name was Tagi something Chang. It was all Chinese to me.

I went to dinner with Tagi the next night and we started dating *professionally*. I offered him a pretty face and companionship and he gave me money and gifts in exchange. It was the perfect love affair. I didn't even have to have sex with him at first. It turned out the guy was more interested in his gambling addiction and loved to take me to the Bicycle club where I learned how to play Texas Hold 'em while he played Pai Gow, a Chinese gambling game.

Whenever Tagi hit it big and was in a good mood he spent hundreds of dollars on me but when he had a bad night, he would do things like yell at me in the parking lot and threaten to kill people. I discovered he had a cocaine addiction on top of his drinking and gambling habits. As much as I wanted to dump him, I preferred to deal with a rich Chinese man with a temper rather than a bunch of slimy men who wanted to rub themselves on me every night at the Hostess Club. It never dawned on me to quit the sex industry completely because where could I go for help? All I knew how to do every single day was survive.

After a while Tagi demanded sex with me so one fateful night we ended up at the Bonaventure Hotel in downtown Los Angeles. He was in his usual bad mood so I tried to get the deed done as soon as possible. When we walked into the elegant room I remember wishing I was on my honeymoon instead. But my life was filled with shattered dreams so I quickly pushed that ridiculous notion out of my head and put sexy white panties on at Tagi's request. Nodding in approval, he put two one hundred-dollar bills in my hand and pulled me onto the bed.

During the two whole minutes we had sex, the condom kept falling off and semen leaked all over me and inside of my body. I jumped off the bed and ran to the bathroom to try and clean myself out. Tagi asked me in his rough Chinese accent, "What's wong?"

What's wrong? Was he kidding? Everything was wrong! I didn't want to get pregnant again from a prostitution act and give birth to some ugly Asian baby. I turned the bath water on and worked feverishly to get any and all bodily fluids off of me. But I had an awful feeling.

Three weeks later when my breasts were swollen and I didn't start my period, I took a pregnancy test and it came back positive. I couldn't believe it. I was so fuming mad at myself.

Questions raced through my mind. How could I let this happen? How am I going to work pregnant? Should I have an abortion? What will my parents say? I didn't know what to do. There was no one to turn to for help. I looked down with tears in my eyes while rubbing my barely pregnant tummy.

I knew I couldn't kill my baby. I still had *some* values from what I'd learned at church. I thought about giving the baby up for adoption but then I'd be left wondering every day if the baby was in a good home. I thought about my parents raising the baby but that thought quickly vanished. So, I made the choice to keep my baby and figure out a way to support us. I couldn't go back to prostitution again. No way. And when I told Tagi he freaked out and threatened to take my baby away. I had to come up with a plan.

It didn't take me long to find a Mexican strip club on the corner of Flower and Figueroa. I was only 18 years old but I had already stolen an I.D. from a girl back at the taxi club when I needed one for gambling. As I walked down the street from my hotel I saw a tall brick building with a flashing neon "TOPLESS" sign on it. I didn't speak much Spanish but the owner didn't seem to mind. He saw a young blonde with green eyes who was 21 years of age and hired me instantly.

At first I loved working at the Mexican strip club. When the Hispanic men saw I could dance like a female Michael Jackson, those dollar bills came flying at me. Unlike most American men, Hispanic men love to be entertained by a good dancer. I did the moonwalk, the splits, grabbed my crotch, and the whole enchilada. As the song "Beat it" came to an end I jumped up on the railing, ripped off my bikini top and threw it into the crowd.

"Olé!"

The Hispanic men *loved* me and called me La Huera Loca, the crazy blonde girl. I made so much money in that club that it was literally falling out of my bikini bottoms! When I went to the restroom to count my "propina" (tips), I sometimes found folded dollar bills with little bags of cocaine inside. I knew it was probably bad for the baby but *just a little* I thought. Exhausted from dancing eight hours a night and being pregnant, I rolled up a dollar bill and snorted a couple of lines.

And then I could *really* dance!

I danced my drug-induced heart out and hustled those hot Hispanic men for three solid months until I became "old meat". Once a girl has worked in a strip club for a few months it's common for men to get bored of her and demand new meat. That's why girls in the sex industry move around so much. That's why porn stars change their names so often. When a girl becomes old meat, we have to come up with new tricks. It's just part of the *game*.

I had an itch for Hollywood so I started looking around on Melrose Boulevard and found a topless club called, "The Last Call." But this club was different than the Mexican club. First of all, the club had a full bar so that meant "drunk stupid men." Secondly, the club had *whiter* clientele so that meant more competition for me. Sure enough I walked in and there were hot blondes and stunning brunettes who were prettier and more experienced than me. Not to mention, I was three months pregnant!

The owner was a little smarter than the last guy and questioned me about my so-called driver's license but of course I lied and he bought my story. By now I was a practiced liar. That's the "norm" for a sex worker. That's why we're called "hustlers." That's why one of the world's most popular adult magazines is called, "Hustler". Need I say more?

Meanwhile I worked up the guts to tell my parents about the upcoming arrival of their first grandchild. I thought they actually might rejoice a little and offer to help me but I was wrong. My mother's cold response was, "Well, if anything happens to you I'm not raising that baby." Her words crushed me. I needed my mother more than I ever did.

I hustled for four more months at the strip club until one night when the owner pulled me aside and told me it was time to go home. I guess my pink fluffy skirt wasn't cutting it anymore. I applied for financial aid from the state of California and received barely enough to pay rent for the dumpy duplex I called home in Huntington Park. I was the only white girl who lived within a ten-mile radius in an all Hispanic neighborhood. It was much cheaper than Hollywood and anyway, I landed there by accident when I agreed to move in with a Mexican girl I met back at the Mexican bar. But I didn't mind. I was La Huera Loca!

After I quit stripping to stay home and be a good wayward pregnant girl, I began preparing for the arrival of my new baby. A friend from the strip club who used to regularly come and visit me offered to buy me some things for the baby. When he showed up at my doorstep with several big shopping bags and a four-foot white teddy bear I was stunned. Nobody had shown me that kind of love in a long time. He also helped me put up baby themed wallpaper and bought me bacon, lettuce and tomato sandwiches whenever I had killer pregnancy cravings, which was about every two hours for six months. Regrettably, I gained 60 pounds thanks to those BLT sandwiches. I often wondered as I stood in front of the mirror how I would support the baby and me. Surely, I thought, my dancing days were over.

Fat, grouchy and tired of having some kid push on my guts for nine months, I went into labor on June 28, 1988. I was in labor for twenty-four hours before I finally delivered my daughter. I started out the day before at my parents' house where I moaned and groaned like a big baby until my mother thought I might actually deliver one. She rushed me to French Hospital in downtown Los Angeles where the doctor calmly told me I was only a few centimeters dilated and to go back home. "What???" This guy was an idiot, I thought. Surely all the pain I was in meant the baby was about to pop out. But he insisted and my mother drove me all the way back to her home in Glendora where several hours later my bag of green water broke on her bed while my 12 year old little brother was sitting next to me. It grossed us both out.

We rushed back to the hospital where I writhed in pain another twelve hours until I finally heard the words, "Push!" and with every ounce of power I had inside of me, I pushed out a big beautiful eight pound and nine ounces baby girl. I pushed so hard that the blood vessels in my eyes popped and I had red eyes for two weeks. It was like someone had pulled off my face and stretched it over my body. The doctor was even amazed at my alien delivery. He had thought for sure that I would need a C-section. He warned me when I was pregnant to lay off the BLT's but I didn't listen.

While the doctor stitched up the huge tear in my birth canal, a nurse holding my daughter quickly bent her over to show me and then rushed her away. My daughter had barely opened her pretty brown eyes to look at me before she was gone. No one explained what was happening and I started to panic.

"What's wrong with my daughter?" I demanded. "I want to hold her!"

"Please calm down, ma'am," said a voice.

They rolled me away to my room where I had to wait several more hours before they let me visit her in the intensive care unit. It turned out the green water that broke was a sign that there was Meconium (baby poo) in my amniotic fluid. They further explained that my baby was experiencing breathing problems because she had inhaled some of the Meconium. My daughter also had Mongolian blue spots on the lower part of her body. When I saw them I immediately blamed myself and later confessed to the doctor that I snorted cocaine the first three months of pregnancy. But the doctor assured me that the spots weren't due to my recreational drug use.

"Actually," he said, "they are common in Asian babies. Is your father's baby Asian?"

Pause.

"Yesss," I replied in a low voice.

I rolled over to the side of the bed with gritted teeth. I really didn't need him to remind me that she was half Asian while I was laying there bleeding and in pain. Every time I heard the word "Asian" I cringed at the thought of Tagi and how I prostituted myself with him.

Several hours later the nurse came in and asked me to sign my daughter's birth certificate. Finally the moment I would announce to the world the beautiful name I had chosen for her. *Tiffany Ann Moore,* I wrote out perfectly and signed the rest until I got to the part where it said, "Father's Name". I stopped writing. There was no way I was going to put Tagi's name on my daughter's birth certificate after he threatened to take my baby away.

The nurse looked at me strangely and said, "You don't know who your baby's father is?" I felt like blurting out, *"No, I do not know who the father is because I am dumb prostitute."*

But I held my tongue and simply replied, "No." The nurse took the certificate and later when she gave it back to me next to Father's Name it read, "Refused to State". Great, I thought, now I'm an official single Mother.

After a traumatizing birth experience and coming home to an empty house, reality entered in and I understood how alone I really was. A 19 year old child raising a child, I had no idea what I was doing and no one to help me. My mother was too far away and the only friends I had were the Mexican ladies who lived next door who barely spoke any English.

"Hola, como estas?" I blurted out holding my new baby. The Mexican ladies loved my daughter Tiffany. They thought she was a little Mexican baby.

"No," I replied. "She's half Asian."

"Ohhh," they answered. If only I had been given a dollar for every time I said that and someone gave me a strange look.

After several months of struggling to be a single Mom and living off of the great state of California, it was finally time for me to go back to work. I called up my old boss at "The Last Call" and told him I had my baby and had lost over sixty pounds and he was thrilled to have me back. My old regulars were still there and showered me with gifts and money to celebrate my great return. I showed off pictures of Tiffany to customers while serving them drinks and giving them table dances. One man flipped out a twenty and asked me to squirt breast milk into his coffee. What a great idea, I thought! So I hustled breast milk squirts for a few months and made a killing since I was the only girl who could do it!

But after a while I became "old meat" again and had to move to another strip club to try and support Tiffany and me. The same vicious cycle repeated itself once again. But this time I swore to myself I would never do prostitution again.

Wait a minute, I said never again, didn't I?

★ *Admit One* ★

★ HELL'S GETAWAY ★

★ *Chapter Six* ★

It was a busy Friday night and the song, "Love Hurts," was playing. A Latina girl was up on the stage dancing while I was over by the front door chatting with Mario, the cute new bouncer on duty. Suddenly, I heard a loud pop and Mario collapsed onto the ground. I threw my tray down and screamed, "Call 911!"

Within seconds people were crowded around Mario trying to stop the bleeding. Girls were screaming all around me.

"Shut up!" I yelled and shoved them into the dressing room. I looked in the mirror and there were streaks of blood on my top.

"Shit, what just happened?"

After a few minutes I ran back out to Mario and saw the paramedics trying to revive him. I prayed silently, "God, please save him." Right before the gunshot Mario was telling me about the new baby his wife just had.

Another girl and I started picking up beer bottles like crazy and dumping ashtrays. I never moved so fast in my life.

Two hours later we got the news from the club manager that Mario was dead. I went home and sat in the dark while holding my bloody bikini top. Thoughts flooded my mind. I felt so bad for Mario and his family. The guy was only twenty-one years old. Then another thought crossed my mind.

It could have been me.

Suddenly an awful feeling gripped me that it was *supposed* to be me. Somebody out there was trying to kill me.

It could have been anyone who pulled that trigger and killed Mario. But I didn't want to stick around and find out so I called up my old Madam, Vanessa, to try and get some "side" work while I looked for another club to dance at. I hated to go back to prostitution but Mario's death was too close of a call for me.

Vanessa was delighted to hear my voice and have me come back to work for her. By then she had a lucrative escort agency and was running about 40 deals a day. So I bought a beeper and started pulling tricks all over Southern California making any-where from $300 to $500 an hour, depending on what the client wanted. I drove all the way down to San Diego and back up to the San Fernando Valley. After a year of hustling men all over Southern California, I thought I was on top of my game.

Through some of my "elite" connections, I began to pursue the Hollywood dream I fantasized about as a child. Like every other sex worker in Southern California, I thought for sure I would become the next Sharon Stone or Julia Roberts.

With Hollywood directors and agents piling up in my pocket, I began to go to casting calls and try out for different acting parts. I became an aspiring "extra." Promises of big breaks made by horny Hollywood directors, I believed them when they told me I would become be a big star. Promises like that were usually made *before* I got down on my knees.

Whenever Hollywood didn't work out I pursued the music industry. One of my regular "guys" was a music producer who had a recording studio in his mansion in Chatsworth. With his help I wrote, sang and produced my first music album in 1991 entitled, "Let There Be House", which included the song, "Mentiroso", I wrote to get back at Mellon Man Ace for "Mentirosa", a Spanglish rap song about female liars.

Maybe I was a little sensitive.

Or maybe I realized my whole life was a huge lie. Rejected, beat up, overworked and overexposed; I was a single Mom surviving a double life. With one foot in the door of Hollywood and the other spiked heel stuck in the sex industry, I felt blocked at every turn. It was as if God Himself was against me.

One day I became so frustrated with the whole LA scene that I began looking for jobs in other cities. Desperately searching for some new angle I stumbled upon an ad in a newspaper:

SEEKING YOUNG WOMEN. ALL TRAVEL EXPENSES PAID. $2,000 A WEEK.

Wow, now *that* sounded good. I immediately called the phone number and some guy Rico answered and told me they were looking for dancers. I was so relieved to hear it wasn't prostitution!

I showed up expecting a professional agency but it was two Mexican men and a briefcase of piles of cash. I had never seen so much cash in my life. They told me there was plenty more for me if I agreed to fly to Mexico to dance for two weeks. I was a little hesitant but they assured me everything was cool.

"Don't worry, Huera, ebery ting is cool. Da girls are makin' a lot a money and da beach is muy bueno."

When I heard my two favorite words "beach" and "money" my eyes brightened. They also promised me a first class ticket and showed me a pamphlet of the beautiful resort where I would be staying. A guy friend of mine warned me that it didn't sound legit but I ignored him. I was ready for a change and needed to take a break from California. Besides, I was La Huera Loca!

I felt bad about leaving my daughter Tiffany but my guy friend assured me she'd be fine. So I grabbed my bags and headed toward the Los Angeles International airport. I took a first class flight on Mexicana airlines and landed in Guadalajara three hours and five minutes later. The smell of tacos and cigarettes filled the air. I grabbed my suitcase and headed outside where two Mexican men pulled up to the side of the curb. I guess the blonde hair gave me away.

"Hola, como estas?" I showed off my Spanish skills as I handed my suitcase to them. I learned quite a bit of Spanish at the Mexican bars I stripped at.

"Hola," one man replied and the rest of the ride it was *very* quiet.

About forty minutes later we arrived at an old building covered by trees and surrounded by Birds of Paradise. I got out of the car and walked up the cracked steps to a secured door. After a short knock a fat Mexican man opened the door and I followed the two men into a corridor of glass sliding doors. Now I *knew* something was wrong. The women behind the glass doors weren't laughing or talking. I noticed out of the corner of my eye a girl wiping what looked like tears off of her face.

What the hell is going on here?

Thoughts of escape immediately filled my mind and I felt my hands turn into fists. When I was about to bash the guy's head in, a Voice came to me and said, "Stay calm, Shelley." I knew it was God. I took in a deep breath and my false smile led me down the hall into my room.

"Be ready by 8:00, Huera," one of the men said as he walked away. I turned around to a striking young woman with long blonde hair and terrified blue eyes.

I looked at her with a puzzled face and blurted, "What the hell is going on here?"

"Shshsh," she said as she shut the door. Then she whispered, "Don't you know where you are? You're in a Mexican brothel."

"Bullshit," I contested. "I didn't sign up to work in a Mexican brothel. And I was told I would be staying in a nice resort!"

"Shut up!" she said. "These guys are going to f—king kill you if you don't shut up. You're in a Mexican brothel and you're not ever going back home."

Stunned, I stood there with my mouth open until I shook my head and boldly came back with, "Well, *nobody* is going to keep me in a prison. That's for damn sure." Then I turned around and stared out the barred window while silently praying to God to get me out of this.

Eight o'clock rolled around and we heard a knock on the door.

"Come on, Hueras. Time to go."

I followed the other girls in a line where we were taken outside to an old yellow bus in the street. Wearing a tight yellow dress and holding nothing but a small purse for tips and tampons, I stepped up into the dirty bus thinking about what was ahead.

"God, get me out of this," I said as the bus pulled away from the curb.

As I looked around at the faces of the other young girls I noticed none of them had emotion. They were as cold as ice staring straight into the view ahead of them. I tried to talk to one of them next to me but she wouldn't speak. I sat back in disbelief as not one of the women had the will to fight. I was such a fighter. I couldn't relate to their submissive behavior and I began to devise a plan to escape.

Luckily, I spoke enough Spanish. I don't think the Mexican mafia planned on that when they lured me in. We arrived at a tall brick building with several floors above it. As I looked to the side I noticed several security guards with guns.

Damn, I thought.

As I stepped out of the dirty yellow bus the air was sticky and hot. Wiping my forehead, I shoved my blonde hair back and walked into a dark empty club where only a few men were sitting at tables. I followed the other girls into a dressing room attached to the stage and poked my head through the curtain. Nobody was watching. It was so weird. It was nothing like the rowdy Mexican bars I was used to.

I wanted to check out the rest of the bar without being noticed so I hopped on the stage and danced quietly while I scouted the area. To the left I saw a girl on a chair dancing for a guy who wasn't tipping her. Not good. To the right I saw the front door guarded by a big Mexican guy who was armed. Very bad. Above me was an open floor where a couple of men were walking around. Where were the women? There were a couple of them on the stage but where were the rest of them?

I asked a Mexican girl in Spanish where the restroom was and she pointed to the floor above me. I escaped out of a window before when a bachelor party got out of hand so I figured it might be an option. I slowly approached the winding stairs and looked above me to see if anyone was around. It was empty so I ran up the stairs and turned to the left where I faced a sign that said, "Baño."

I hurried over to the restroom when a sound stopped me dead in my tracks.

"Nooo!" a woman's voice shrieked out of nowhere.

Oh shit, I thought. *What was that?*

I walked toward the sound of repeated screams and peered in the doorway to see a woman bent over with a handful of men watching while a man behind her violently thrust himself into her.

"No, no more," she pleaded and the guy slapped her on the head and said, "cierra la boca." Okay, he just told her to shut her mouth after he hit her. That was enough for me to see.

I *knew* I was in hell.

I immediately walked to the restroom to see if I could crawl out of the window onto the roof. But there were no windows. I panicked. I went into a stall to sit and think. Thoughts of ways to escape the hell I was in flooded my mind.

Maybe I could ask for a match and start a fire? Not good enough.

I could bullshit the doorman and pretend to give him a blow job and steal his gun. Mmmm, there was no guarantee that would work.

I could pretend I was demon possessed and twist my head around like the exorcist. No, they would kill me for sure.

Damn, I was out of ideas. So I sat there and prayed and begged God to get me out of this. He had been successful many times at saving me, so I thought maybe He'd forgive me this one last time. But there was no answer. Tears rolled down my face as I thought about my daughter and how I'd never see her again. I was beyond despair.

Cries from another woman filled the air and I became desperate. I talked myself into the doorman idea. I would have done any sexual favor to get out of that hell hole. As I walked toward the doorman my quick thinking Spanish kicked in and I grabbed his arm in desperation and yelled, "Fuego! Fuego! Hay un fuego ahí arriba!" He looked at me in shock and ran upstairs to see the fire I had yelled about.

I speedily ran out the door and down the street trying to wave cars down as they drove by. A green taxi cab slowed down and pulled over to the curb. I told him in Spanish to take me back to the brothel and he understood what I was talking about. Thank God he knew where it was. Thank God my Spanish was good enough.

During the cab ride I mentally prepared myself to face the security guard at the brothel. I thought about the door, the lock, his desk, the sliding glass doors, how long it would take me to bust in and get my stuff.

No sooner had we arrived and I was ready to kick some serious ass. Filled with the will to live and see my daughter again, I threw a twenty-dollar bill at the driver and told him to wait five minutes and I'd give him a hundred American dollars when I got back. He nodded.

I ran up to the steps and pounded on the front door where the security guard opened it and I shoved him back while I rushed down the corridor to my room on the left. The sliding glass doors were locked. Shit!

I turned and yelled, "Abierto el f—king door!" He tried to tackle me but I shoved him into the wall and kicked him brutally until he gave me the keys. He wasn't ready for a trained stripper with legs of steel to kick the hell out of him. I ran to my room and stuck several keys into the hole and bam, I felt a click.

Got it.

I grabbed my suitcase and tore out of the room toward the front door where I leaped over the stairs to the cab. Thank God he was still there. With the door slammed behind me I told the driver to take me to the Guadalajara International Airport. My heart was beating rapidly while I suffered through a forty-minute drive to the airport.

Tears of relief flowed down my face as I stepped out of the cab and ran inside to the airlines desk. I lied and said my daughter was sick and I needed to change my flight to get home immediately. I sat down in the chair directly across from the desk gripping tightly to my purse. I wasn't going to let anything stop me from going back to Los Angeles.

After a sleepless night in the airport and a three-hour flight I stepped off of the plane and onto American soil and kissed the ground. Thank God I was home. Thank God I was alive.

I was so traumatized after Mexico that I slept for three straight days. When I woke up I swore off prostitution and headed back to the club where Mario was killed. It had been a while since I worked there so hopefully the murderer was caught. Anyway, I needed the money. A hot blonde with Spanish on my tongue and Tequila in my veins, I'd make a killing.

"Olé!"

★ *Admit One* ★

★ **DEAD EVEN** ★

★ *Chapter Seven* ★

I was out for blood.

That psycho was going to regret the night he ever met me. When I came home and found him sitting on my couch with a huge knife, I was furious.

"What are you doing here, Miguel?" I demanded to know. He didn't answer me except with the sound of heavy breathing and rocking back and forth on my couch. I quickly handed my three-year old daughter to my roommate and motioned her towards the bedroom.

"Lock it and don't open it unless you hear my voice." I said. Adrenaline rushed into my veins.

I'm going to kill him, I told myself. *I'm going to cut him into little pieces and hurl them into the dumpster across the street.* But something told me to play it cool. If I killed him I'd probably end up in jail. Or worse, he might hurt my daughter Tiffany. No, this guy required "special" handling.

"Sweetie," I said as I changed my tone. "I love you, Miguel. Put the knife down, honey. I'm sorry I got home so late but it was my turn to clean up the bar." My loving eyes welcomed him back into my open arms. His face softened along with the grip around his knife.

That night I stayed up until 5:00 a.m. convincing Miguel that I loved him more than any other man. I did whatever it I had to do to protect Tiffany and me. For months the maniac had been harassing me and stalking me. I should have recognized he was a stalker the first night I met him but the money blinded me. All I saw was a mountain of green in front of me. His big brown eyes and boyish smile, Miguel was every stripper's dream: a young *rich* good-looking man.

The first night I met Miguel he gave me a crystal rose and $500 in tips along with a request for dinner the following night. I told him I had to work but he offered to pay me *double* what I usually made. I greedily accepted and blindly entered into one of the worst episodes of my crazy life.

It started off perfect. He spoiled me with money and gifts and I spoiled him with sex and soft talk. He had no idea that I was stringing along several other men at the same time I was stringing him along. Not to mention my lesbian babysitter. I was a professional hustler by then and didn't have the heart to love anyone. I wanted the money; cold hard ready dirty cash. Besides, any man who came into a strip club and expected a stripper to be faithful to him deserved to be strung along.

That was my mentality.

After two weeks Miguel began to act jealous and start fights with my regulars at the bar. That was a very big no-no for me.

I explained to him that he wasn't paying my bills and had no right to disrupt my business but he insisted I belonged to him and that he would kill any man who came near me. I told him to leave immediately but he flipped up my tray and threw a chair over. It turned out he was a crazy Ecuadoran and a practiced Tequila drinker. I had met my match.

I really thought I had dated some weirdos in my day but this guy took the cake. No matter what I did, I couldn't get rid of him. I tried begging him in tears. It didn't work. I tried telling him I had a disease. He didn't care if he caught it from me. I lied and said a family member died and I needed time to grieve. But when he came into the club and saw me laughing that story died. I finally had to ask the men at the bar to help me get rid of him. They agreed and ganged up on him near his apartment and threatened him. He wasn't affected by it all. He was impenetrable. He was a complete unmodified psycho. In fact, I called him "slasher" for short because he slashed not only my tires but any other person's tires that came near me. He was relentless.

After I refused to take his calls or speak to him anymore, he began to make death threats on a daily basis. I called the police to complain but when they asked me where I worked I hung up the phone. No cop was going to listen to a stripper.

One night I borrowed a neighbor's motorcycle to drive to work because the "slasher" had struck again and slashed all four of my tires. As I pulled out of the driveway and looked around carefully, there was no one around as I sped off to work. About five minutes later I heard the sounds of a revved up truck engine gaining on me and I *knew* it was him. I looked over my left shoulder and there was the psycho yelling at me out the window.

"Pull over, Giovanna," he called me by my stage name. "Pull over right now. I want to talk to you." I ignored him. I kept driving forward hoping he would follow me all the way to the nearest police station. A second later I saw his Toyota truck veering into my lane and I figured it was to try and scare me but no, that psycho rammed his blue truck right into my motorcycle! I flipped up in the air and off the bike, landing in a huge ivy bush.

I hurt so badly but I didn't care. Terrified, I got up and ran as fast as I could through backyards and bushes until I finally came to a lighted back porch. A man came out and saw the blood and bumps on me and called 911. The cops came and took a police report and my friend's motorcycle got towed away to the junkyard.

Great, I thought. My friend's motorcycle was trashed.

Miguel never caught me that night but he did give me some bruises and bumps to think about. I kept a low profile for a few days while my body healed. It gave me some time to think. I had to come up with a plan to get rid of him forever.

A week had gone by and not a word from Miguel. I figured he was freaked out by the accident because he was probably drunk when he did it. Besides, there was a hit and run out on him and he was headed straight for jail. Or so I thought.

He got arrested about a week later but it was thrown out of court. When a kind and courteous Miguel told the judge I was a stripper, it was all over for me. I stomped out of court in disbelief. I couldn't believe the judge "judged" me like that. There was nothing I could say or do and I felt betrayed and hopeless.

Friday night came along and it was my turn to clean up after closing time. I stacked up the dancers' trays and wiped down the entire bar. I was really tired and couldn't wait to go to bed. My friend Justin gave me a ride home that night and we stopped off to pick up my daughter Tiffany and my roommate at a friend's house. It was about 2:45 a.m.

As we walked toward our apartment I grabbed my keys and unlocked the front door. Exhausted from work, I didn't notice the screen lying on the ground near my feet. When I opened the door I was shocked to see a man sitting on my couch with a knife. Miguel!

That was it for me. He had pushed me over the edge and into insanity. Later that day I called up Justin and we devised an evil plan. Justin loved me and would have done anything for me. And he did.

Everything was set. Justin waited in the parking lot while I stood outside of a restaurant near my home. Miguel took the bait and showed up thirty minutes after me. I knew he couldn't show up earlier than that because he was married with kids. I would have told his wife about our "psycho" affair but I always felt sorry for the kids. *But not tonight,* I thought. I didn't care if those kids ever saw their father again.

Miguel suspected I was up to something and guarded everything he said or did. He was extremely smart, *when he was sober.* So I suggested we do shots of Tequila for "old times' sake."

There had been so much blood spilt between us and I just wanted it to end, I told him as I softly laid my hand on his. I knew I could melt his heart. I also knew he was carrying a gun. We drank about ten shots together, or at least he did. I gulped my shot back and threw each one behind my ear. While he got drunk I slipped a bag of "extra" cocaine into his pocket. I knew he dabbled in cocaine and hoped he still had some in his system.

After an hour or so I asked him if I could use the restroom. He argued I was trying to set him up and I insisted I really had to go. I walked around the corner and found the nearest payphone and called 911.

"Please help me. I'm being held hostage at a bar by a man with a gun. We're sitting in the booth near the front door," I cried on the phone.

Ten minutes later the cops busted in and searched Miguel and found a gun on him and a little bag of cocaine in his right pocket. Miguel's eyes fumed into mine as they handcuffed him and placed him under arrest. After a few minutes I walked by the cop car and smiled at Miguel through the glass dangling his truck keys in front him. Oh yeah, I forgot to mention I stole those out of his jacket pocket.

Miguel was arrested and charged with carrying a concealed weapon and drug possession and sentenced to one month in jail. While he rotted behind county bars, I happily rode off in his 4x4 truck to enjoy the sandy beaches in Ensenada, Mexico.

Two weeks later I returned Miguel's sandy truck to the Los Angeles County Jail parking lot and left his keys and a good riddance note on the front tire.

Go to hell, psycho, I thought to myself as I adjusted my rear view mirror. A sense of evil staring back at me, I noticed a slight smile tugging at my lips.

Hmmm, was that a psycho on my face?

★ Admit One ★

★ PSYCHO STRIPPER ★

★ Chapter Eight ★

I became a bona fide insane sexual psychopath.

A survivor of years of verbal and physical abuse from men, unwanted pregnancies, drugs and alcohol, homelessness, near death experiences, attempted rapes, a daring escape from Mexico and as of late, a psycho boyfriend, I had completely lost my mind and heart to the soul sucking sex industry. Any last piece of "Shelley" that was left was my stubborn will to survive.

I continued the vicious cycle of sex work and tried my luck *again* in Hollywood. I was burned out from the crazy Hispanic environment of flying beer bottles and Mariachi mamas so I attempted to settle down into the dull boring world of sleazy white men.

Sunset Boulevard in Hollywood was called "The Strip" for more than a few reasons. Besides being the most famous street for rock and roll clubs, rocker restaurants and the rock walk, Sunset was also known for its beautiful strippers: hot, long-legged sexy blonde strippers. I hated working there.

First of all, I didn't have big boobs. I was a natural "B" cup while every woman around me was at least a "D" cup. Natural or not, boobs mattered to men, especially white men. Mexican men were more attracted to personality, looks and performance, although a curved backside was a plus.

But white men didn't like me very much. I was a crazy white girl who could dance, not some floozy who put on a ten-dollar peep show. I couldn't stand still long enough to give anyone a peep show. Okay, sure, I gave customers a little peek-a-boo once in a while for the right amount of cash, but other than that I was an "interpretive" dancer, not a floor whore.

Denial enters.

The strip clubs in Hollywood were worse than prostitution as far as I was concerned. Seedy and quiet, sleazy cheap men hung dollar bills over the side of the stage to get a worm's-eye view of a naked woman spreading her legs. To make things worse, women wrapped their exposed bodies around stripper poles with God knows how many vaginal fluids we all had to share!

Yuck!

I just couldn't stomach the Hollywood strip clubs. They were dirty, sleazy and a breeding ground for disease. Not to mention, the competition was stiffer than the drinks. Hollywood blonde hopefuls lined up at the bar every night with their long beautiful hair and large breasts. There was no way to make money, especially on a Friday night when fifty girls showed up to work. I was lucky if I even danced one set before the night was over. In order to make money in these clubs, girls had to be absolutely gorgeous *or* hustle drinks, offer peeks at their privates and give a hand job or two where applicable. No, the Hollywood strip clubs weren't for me. I might as well go back to prostitution if I was going to put on peep shows for dollar bills. What other choice did I have?

Frustrated, I walked by a newspaper stand one day and saw the *LA Xpress* paper through the glass. A plethora of sexy ads, I browsed through hundreds of women offering massage, private dances, companionship and more.

Hmmm, it was so tempting, I thought.

The low voice interrupted my thoughts, "and the men would come to you and you wouldn't have to work as hard. You would have more freedom."

I argued back in my head, "yeah, but it's extremely illegal. I could go to prison for running a prostitution house."

The small voice overrode mine, "but you're too smart to get busted. You've never been caught before, Shelley."

So I agreed with the voice, whoever it was. I was so crazy and intoxicated most of the time I didn't even notice when I was talking to myself.

The following month I got an 800 number and worked up the nerve to go down to the *LA Xpress* building on La Brea where I submitted an ad with a huge picture of me and some girl fondling each other. *Oh yeah,* I thought. My ad was definitely going to get noticed.

And I was right. My phone was ringing off the hook.

"Hello," I answered in a sexy voice. A man on the other end, I spoke softly to him, "Why thank you. Yes, *of course* you can have two girls. Yes, it's $300 an hour per girl. Sure, sweetie, we can do *that.* I can't wait to meet you either."

By now I was a *proven* hustler.

I was also a raging alcoholic, drug user, horrible mother and suicidal. Sure, I was good at hiding it because I had built up powerful defense mechanisms over the years. I was an expert at denial. I was also a nineteen-year veteran liar fluent in English *and* Spanish, not to mention some Italian, Arabic, Chinese, Japanese and whatever else language the hundreds of men I slept with spoke. Oh yeah, I made my rounds. I was a hooker in Los Angeles, home to one of the largest multi-ethnic populations in the world, where I became an expert in matters of culture, drugs, nightlife, prostitution and men.

In fact, I became more of a counselor to men at the end of my career than an actual prostitute. I listened for 45 minutes while they bashed their wives or complained about their bosses and then I gave them advice and stuck my hand out for payment. I admit I was the last person who should have given advice but remember, I was in denial.

I lived a crazy, indecent, unsanitary, indescribable life. Jack Daniels regularly in my veins, one of the craziest things I ever did was drive topless during the day with the convertible top down. When a cop pulled me over in my red Miata for drunk driving, I performed the "walk-and-turn" DUI test perfectly. I was a stripper for crying out loud. When he proceeded to test my motor skill abilities, I blurted out the alphabet backwards faster than any human being alive. I thought I was invincible. And I was out to prove it to the world.

Until one fateful night, when I was finishing up a shopping day with a sugar daddy, and saw cop cars all around my apartment building. I *knew* they were for me. I instructed my sugar daddy (slave) to do exactly as I said and to pretend to be my husband and that Tiffany was our daughter.

We approached my apartment cautiously and blamelessly, of course. I was a married woman now with child. I had to play the part.

"Hello, excuse me, officer, what is going on?" I humbly asked as I entered my apartment.

"Ma'am, are you the occupant of this apartment?"

"Yes, sir, my husband, my daughter and I live here," I said as I gracefully stepped onto the front door mat. "I don't understand, officer, is there something wrong?" I leaned in closer with a sincere look of concern.

"Ma'am, do you run a massage agency here?" the cop asked me straight out.

Damn, I thought. I immediately responded. "Of course not. Why would you ask us that?"

"Well, there's a girl upstairs who was tied and raped at gunpoint in your bed and she claims you run a massage agency here."

That stupid bitch, I cursed in my mind. She was going to get me busted!

But filled with the will to see the sun rise again, I explained to the kind officer that my husband and I were embarrassed but we picked up the young woman at a strip bar the night before when she explained to us she had nowhere to stay. It was only supposed to be for the night, we told the officer. Luckily, he believed my story but I never wanted to live that close to the edge again. So I stopped taking calls for a while.

Maybe I'll go back to the strip club, I thought.

And the vicious cycle repeated itself.

History also repeated itself. I ended right back at the *first* strip club I auditioned at when I was seventeen years old. In the 80s it was called, "Top Hat" but the club changed owners and now the flashing sign read, "Illusions".

How ironic, I thought as I stood there beneath the sign. My life had become the greatest illusion on earth where I performed the same horrible act over and over again.

A trained seal, I walked through the familiar red curtained entrance into the strip club circus to perform my final act.

IX

★ *Admit One* ★

★ DEATH DEFYING ★

★ *Chapter Nine* ★

There was never a time for me to check out. It was 1992 and I was still stuck in the sex industry. A lovely face in an ugly place, I could never fix the broken record of my life's song, "Hotel California." Every time the DJ played that song, which was every night, I was slapped in the face with the harsh reality: I was stuck in the sex industry and there was no way out.

No matter how hard I cried or how many times I prayed through the years, God didn't answer. I must have been utterly unforgivable, I thought.

With no ability to care about myself or anything else, I continued my death-defying act at Illusions strip club. With a Jack and Coke in one hand and a cigarette in the other, I danced my heart, mind and health away. My condition was worsening and I could barely stand up straight some nights. Customers saw me falling apart but they ignored my pain and continued to contribute to my demise.

"Giovanna, whadda ya drinking?"

"Jack and Coke," I replied and pulled out a cigarette.

Men didn't care about me. They only cared if the object I had become was fueled regularly for performance.

I guzzled my drink down.

"Another drink, Giovanni?" asked a burly voice.

"Sure," I said as I wiped my mouth and slid my glass across the bar. "Thanks, babe." I turned around into my familiar dark surroundings to seek out my next naive victim. It was a Friday night and self-seeking married men were everywhere. The shiny reflections of their wedding rings reinforced the bitter truth I held so dearly: men could never *ever* be trusted.

With money on my mind and alcohol on my brain, I heard my name over the loudspeaker.

"Hey Gents, let's give a nice sexy warm welcome for one of our hottest dancers, Geeeeoooovanni!"

It was my turn to dance. The final week for this month's hottest dancer contest, I was sure I would win. Although I had won second or third a couple times in the past, I never failed to place. It was unthinkable. I was damn good and I knew it.

Dom dom da, da diga dom dada. Dom dom da, da diga dom dada.

The beat of the music summoned me and I felt my body crumble under the hot red lights. As I began to roll around the floor like a wild animal in heat, every man's eyes were on me. The devilish beats as my guide, I slithered across the floor towards my victims and seduced them, every single one of them.

"Wanting. Needing. Waiting, for you, to justify my love."

Madonna's illustrious sex song ended. Nobody made a sound. There was no applause. They knew they had been placed under a spell and there was no way out. Full of a lust for power, I effortlessly walked off the stage toward the bar to suck on another drink.

"Jack and Coke," I said as I puffed on my cigarette with a curved smile. I was so entirely arrogant. That's why when they announced the winner and it wasn't me, I was mortified.

"What???" I turned my head. I couldn't believe it. The judges picked Mina, the short fat Latin girl. Tears of frustration and rejection filled my eyes and I ran to the bathroom. My lesbian roommate tried to talk to me through the door but I didn't want to listen anymore. I was done. I hated my life so much that if I couldn't even win a dance contest anymore, I was going to end it.

Later that night I went home and recklessly searched for any and all prescription pills I could get my hands on. Hormone pills, stomach medicines, Tylenol, sleeping pills, mixed with alcohol and meth amphetamine, I was dead serious about killing myself.

"Do it, Shelley. Nobody cares. Nobody loves you. Do it!" pleaded the sinister voice.

The voice was right. Nobody loved me. Nobody cared about me. I was a throw-away person that nobody wanted. Six long years of living daily in pain and suffering, I was done. I swallowed the handfuls of pills with gulps of Bacardi and laid back on my soft white comforter. It was just a matter of time, I hoped. In tears, I whispered sweet good-byes to my daughter Tiffany.

"Mommy loves you. I'm sorry I was such a bad mommy. Someone will come to take care of you. Don't worrrr..." I passed out.

Thirty minutes later I felt someone shaking me. I opened my eyes and saw little creatures running up and down my curtains. My head was pounding and I felt a terrible buzzing in my teeth. Suddenly a horrific image of an Asian faced slug creature with huge long fangs appeared next to me with hordes of little black demons chomping on its flesh. I was completely out of my mind. My girlfriend dragged me to the car and rushed me to the hospital where they pumped my stomach out.

Several hours later I woke up with a very sore throat staring at the same little creatures I saw on my curtains.

A woman walked in with a notepad and started asking me questions. I answered her:

"No, I am not suicidal."

"Yes, I have a daughter."

"No, I did not try to kill myself. I think someone slipped drugs into my drink."

Liar.

I left the hospital later that day pissed off that I didn't die. Why the hell did God let me live? What, so I can survive another day in a hell-hole?

Back to performing the same horrible act, I rotted away in the strip club for several more months until I met Samantha, from Hollywood. She was a witchy looking woman with dark brown hair and sensuous red lips. I noticed her staring at me out of the corner of her eye. When I finished my set and walked off the stage, she motioned me to come over to her.

"You are such a hot dancer," she whispered into my ear.

That night we spent several hours talking and drinking together. She was a bi-sexual woman and was interested in money as much as she was sex with women. I told her how sick I was of the strip club and how prostitution almost killed me. She told me she knew a better and safer way to make money, and that it was legal.

Porn?

"Yeah, and you can make $2,000 a movie."

"Wow." I sat back and sipped on my Jack Daniels. That was a lot of money for a suicidal single mother who was burned out from strip clubs and prostitution.

"That is hell a lot of money," resonated the low voice.

So I hung up my stripper boots, flew to Utah to get breast implants and bravely entered into the world of porn where I performed my greatest flea circus act yet: Roxy, the porn star.

★ *Admit One* ★

★ ACT III ★

★ *Meet Roxy the Porn Star* ★

★ *Admit One* ★

★ ROXY'S REVENGE ★

★ *Chapter Ten* ★

"Oh, yeah," I moaned as a blonde woman I'd never met before groped my body and licked my face. I was so full of shit. By now I was a *proficient* liar.

I was also liquored up and scared stiff. I'll never forget the day I performed in my first amateur porn scene. Dressed in a white leather mini-skirt with bleached blonde hair, I pushed open two red doors and entered into a pitch black room filled with smoke. Overwhelmed by a feeling that I was walking into something more than just a little sex in front of a camera, I stopped dead in my tracks.

Oh, God, I thought. *What the hell am I getting myself into?*

I could barely see a man in the back waving me to come over to him. My eyes were fixed on the well-lighted corner where I saw a camera with a wide angle lens staring at a sexy purple couch and a box of Baby Wipes.

Gulp.

I couldn't shake the "dark" feeling all around me. Everything felt wrong. I tried to turn back but something powerful drew me in. A man's loud voice interrupted my thoughts. "Hey, are you the Blonde sent over by Samantha?"

I walked over to the creepy man holding a cigarette and answered carefully, "Yeah, I'm her."

His eyes licked me up and down as I handed him my AIDS test. "You'll do just fine," he said. He shifted his weight forward and asked, "What's your porn name, honey?"

Uh . . . that's a good question. Well, I partied last night at the Roxy in Hollywood, I thought. So yeah, I'll call myself Roxy. He nodded when I told him my new name and I wondered where I could find a bathroom to down some Jack.

A naked woman, blonde and sexy, walked into the room. Her purple pumps clicked as she came toward me. "I can't wait," she said, eyes on my flesh. "Our scene is next. You're with me."

Jack, I thought. *I need Jack now.*

I hurried my way to the back where I saw G-strings and sex toys thrown on the floor in a worn out room where naked girls were changing. The bathroom was in the back, but I didn't want people to think I was a baby for changing alone. So I walked to a corner in the room, looked around to make sure no one was watching, and took a huge gulp of Jack Daniels. The smell of sex and alcohol filled my nose.

"I can't believe I'm doing this," I said to myself, chasing my words with another gulp of Jack Daniels.

But prostitution and stripping almost killed me, I reasoned. Anyway, porn was legal.

I downed some more Jack and wiped my mouth with the back of my hand.

"Okay, everyone," shouted a guy from the other room. "Time to shoot."

Oh shit, I thought. I fastened my red bra, took another swig, then hurried out of the room to the couch where two porn stars were sitting. I was scared to death.

"You can do this, Shelley," I lied to myself as I straightened my skirt and my fake smile led me over to the couch. Thoughts raced through my mind. How the hell should I greet someone I was about to have sex with?

"Hey, I'm Roxy and I'll be having sex with you."

"Hi, nice to meet you. I guess we're having sex today."

Okay, that's weird.

I practiced the words in my mind but it was too late and I was standing next to the camera before I knew it. Purple-pump-girl and some airhead blonde giggled as the director told us the scene was about a professor who was going to teach naughty college girls how to get an "A".

How stupid, I thought.

The director proudly finished explaining his Academy Award winning scene with a loud clap and, "Let's do it."

Okay, Spielberg.

Lights, camera, action. We were off. And apparently the crew wanted to get off, too. Most of them had their hands down their pants as the scene started. I noticed out of the corner of my eye as the blonde girl started baby talking to the professor about how she needed a good lesson.

This is ridiculous, I thought.

The terrible acting blonde girl went on and on about her bad grades and then pointed to me saying she had a friend who needed a lesson too. Wrong. I would be the one to teach them a lesson. Filled with Jack Daniels and a renewed zeal, I grabbed the girl by the neck and showed them my version of the scene. The director loved it.

"Wow, Roxy, you're so hot. Keep going, baby." The fleshy director fed my starved ego. "Mmmm. ... you could be the next biggest porn star with talent like that."

Random thoughts bounced around in my mind. I loved it. I hated it. I loved the attention. I loved the camera. I hated that I had to have some stupid girl's tongue in my mouth. Yuck.

At that moment a very dark presence came over me.

"I'll make you famous and everyone will love you," the familiar voice hissed. The presence was so thick it made me look around to see if anyone was there. Suddenly a powerful urge to be the best and destroy everyone in my path overwhelmed me.

Rage rose up. Years and years of rage against my father and all the men who ever hurt me washed over me. I ravaged my blonde victim like a wild animal out for innocent blood.

She was no match for my wrath as I shoved her off of the couch. Her mascara smeared eyes looked up at me in fear while she lay there holding the red marks on her arms.

Suddenly the director interrupted, "Okay, I need the money shot. Face to the camera, Roxy. Show me your killer eyes."

"The professor" pulled out of the other blonde and ejaculated all over my face while I pretended to love every minute of it. The taste of bitter fluid and degradation filled my mouth. Suddenly shame and guilt swept over me just like when I was a little girl. Fighting the urge to cry, I turned my head to sniff up my tears.

"Beautiful, Roxy. What a shot," the director said as he clapped. Then some guy threw the Baby Wipes at me. I wanted to die.

I wiped the "professor's" goo off of my face cursing his name under my breath. I didn't want *anyone* to see my pain. No way would I let them see me suffer.

When I looked up the director was already talking about the next scene. What happened to me being the next big porn star?

The director gave me a card, paid me, and then told me to go meet Bobby.

Cash in my purse, Jack in my veins, wrath in my heart I was determined to become the next big porn star. I'd prove everyone wrong and get back at all the men who ever hurt me. And I'd make them pay.

Fame, fortune and sweet revenge.

★ *Admit One* ★

★ **USED AND ABUSED** ★

★ *Chapter Eleven* ★

With a hunger for money and a lust for revenge, I soon took the plunge into professional porn films. Not long after my first porn scene I showed in up in Van Nuys where I caught the eye of top porn producer, Bobby Hollander.

"What a beautiful pair of hips," a man with an open neck shirt and gold chain greeted me. He looked like he was in the Mafia. I played it cool and told him so-and-so had sent me and he nodded. He invited me to sit on his lap where he gently instructed me on how to further my "modeling" career. He was one of the most affectionate men I had ever met.

"Roxy, you have beautiful hips. I want you to be in my new movie."

I told him I would do it but that I still had my heart set on professional acting and modeling. "Sure, baby, you're a pretty girl. But porn can help you get into Hollywood."

I trusted him. Tender and encouraging, he was like a father to me.

I showed up on the set of my first "real" porn movie in 1993. When I walked in through the doors of a luxury home, I was a nervous wreck. Bobby tried to soothe me and make me feel comfortable.

"Hey everybody, this is Roxy. She's a new rising star," Bobby said as he put his arm around me. Peter North smiled at me.

"Hi, everyone." I was at a loss for words. It was hard to keep a straight face while shaking hands with naked porn stars in broad daylight.

"Hey Bobby, where's the restroom?" I asked in desperation.

"It's there in the back to the left, doll." He pointed towards the hall.

"Great, thanks." I quickly walked to the bathroom, shut the door, locked it and pulled out some Vodka. Gulp. I stopped and stared at myself in the mirror.

I can't go through with this, I thought.

A knock on the door woke me out of my daze and I answered, "Yes?"

"Hey Roxy, did you get your enema?"

Oh God, I worried. *Did she just say enema?*

I took another swig and answered back, "Uh, no, why would I need one of those?"

"It's for the dildo scene."

Gulp. I guzzled the vodka down until I worked up enough nerve to come out of the bathroom.

Filled with liquid courage I walked across the hall to where the women were changing. Thank God their scene was before mine because it gave me some time to think. Staring at an empty corner, I sensed another Person in the room with me.

What was He doing here?

Damn, I thought. The last thing I wanted was for Jesus to visit me on a porn set. No thanks. I grabbed my Vodka and guzzled it down. Then I reminded Him that He wasn't paying my bills; I had to do what I had to do.

"Shelley, please don't do this. I have something better for you," a Voice whispered.

"God, please leave me alone. I have to do this." I turned my head in shame and the pain began to surface. I pulled up my nylons, ignored my pain and walked out of the room.

With a little help from Vodka and a whole lot of help from *Liar*, I entered into one of the most traumatizing moments of my career. The last thing I remember is gritting my teeth while Nikki Sinn used and abused me with a spiked dildo.

I wanted to die.

I swore to myself that would be the last porn film I made and I called up old Hollywood contacts. A part for a harem girl opened up so I immediately took off to Los Angeles.

When I arrived to the audition there were hundreds of other girls just like me. Out of several hundred women, only 250 of us got the part as naked harem girls in the movie, "Don Juan Demarco". When the chain smoking Johnny Depp walked by to enjoy the scenery, I pointed to him and blurted out, "Hey, why does he get to smoke?"

He looked at me like I was crazy and walked away leaving a cloud of smoke behind him. I didn't care what he thought. I was the one who had to work in the buff for eight hours on a non-smoking set.

Whenever Hollywood didn't work out and I became desperate for cash, I fell back into porn. I hated the thought of having some man's bodily fluids on my face so I tried to only do girl/girl lesbian scenes. Even though I wasn't a wholehearted lesbian, I could definitely fake an orgasm. Prostitution taught me that.

My first lesbian scene I was really nervous, especially when I saw the American flag on a bedspread. Guilt swept over me when a flashback to 1976 reminded me that I bought a bicentennial plate for my mother. I was such a patriotic little girl back then. But that girl didn't exist anymore, I told myself.

When the camera started rolling the first words out of my mouth were, "I don't think I can do this." Giggling to play the part of a first time lesbian, it helped to hide my extreme embarrassment. When the camera zoomed in and focused on me, I really felt pressure to perform.

"Hi, I'm Roxy," I tried to sound like Marilyn Monroe. I was actually a chain smoker with a worn out raspy voice. I was so embarrassed.

Suddenly the director moved the camera to the other girl's belly button. When I looked over there was a dog sniffing her leg. I couldn't believe it.

What a scum sucking deal this is, I thought.

I wanted to get the scene over with so I made a move to show off the girl's sexy tattoo. But when I pulled her garter to the side, I was shocked to see a Cross on her hip. She said it was a "God-given" thing but it was a hell of a sign for me.

I tried to shake the awful feeling and focus on the scene but the damn tattoo was a reminder of Who was also in the room.

God, I need a drink, I thought.

The evil inside of me was aroused and it gave me strength to finish the scene. Within seconds I was transformed into a wild animal, an entirely different person than the nervous girl in the beginning. A ravenous pig throughout, the scene ended with me licking myself.

I went home to Jack Daniels that night and washed all my guilt and filth away. I hated how foul I smelled after making porn.

A week later I showed up on the same set and desecrated the American flag once again. Only this time I gave in and degraded myself with a man. I wondered if the bedspread had been washed.

The word spread quickly that a new "energetic" double D blonde had hit the porn scene and I started getting phone calls.

"Roxy, I need you for a movie with Dave Hardman."

"Roxy, this is Rodney Moore. I'm a friend of Bobby's."

"Roxy, I need you for a double D scene."

"Hey Roxy, I'll put you on the front cover of my movie if you do an anal scene."

No anal, I promised myself. I had already given into pressure by porn producers to do scenes with men. That was bad enough. Enduring hours of dirty sets, filthy men and their horrible body odors was way beyond my limit. I couldn't imagine one of these dirty men penetrating me anally. It was unthinkable. I hadn't even done that in prostitution.

Luckily, the fake boobs gave me an edge and I could avoid the unthinkable for a while. I also discovered that I could make money as a porn star prostitute. One of the top porn producers I worked for offered me big money to give "privates" to high dollar clients.

"Roxy, now that your movies are out in adult theatres, fans will pay top dollar to spend time with you."

I hated the idea of doing prostitution again but I hated porn even more. When I was offered $2,500 to spend a weekend with a rich lawyer, I reluctantly agreed and took the next flight out to Phoenix where I met Howard, the meth addict.

A whole weekend on meth almost killed me. Not only could Howard "go" for hours but he wouldn't shut up. Not to mention he refused to wear a condom. I tried everything I could think of to make him wear it but he reminded me of the large sum of money I was being paid. When I called up my new "pimp" to complain he said, "Don't worry, he's clean."

How the hell does he know if he's clean, I thought.

When I returned from Arizona I slept for two straight days. After a terrible hangover and $2,500 in cash, I wasted my money on shoes, bras, boas and booze. When I showed up to work with my purple suitcase, I looked like every other jaded porn star. Worn out, wasted and just wanted to get the damn scenes over with.

Damn, I wish this guy would hurry up and cum, I thought.

Damn, I felt so used and abused.

★ *Admit One* ★

★ HUMAN HELL ★

★ *Chapter Twelve* ★

"Harder, f—k me harder!" I viciously screamed back.

The vulgar words shot out of my mouth as I was forcefully and anally penetrated by a brutal male performer. When screaming wasn't enough to endure the pain, I stuffed another man's penis into my mouth like a human pacifier. The sucking helped relieve the pain. Breathing deeply through my nostrils, the stench of bodily fluids filled my burning lungs. Rotten, dirty foul anal smells; I was in a human hell.

I couldn't get out of it. There was no crying allowed. I saw what happened to other girls who cried and wrecked scenes. I wasn't going to get yelled at or worse, punched in the face.

Besides, this was my chance to prove to the world that I was the best.

So I took the stabbing pain. Hard, fast and furious I screamed myself through the violent thrusts.

"F—k me, f—k me!" I yelled louder.

F—k them, I thought! No damn man could *ever* hurt me. I swore it with every violent thrust. Nothing they could do to me would have an effect on me. Filthy wild pigs, they were nothing but poles I used to pay my bills. Gritting my teeth in denial, the powerful lies in my head repeated to the slapping sound of each violent thrust.

Slap, slap, slap, slap, slap.

Take it, Shelley. Take the pain. Show them you can take it. Breathe, just breathe, Shelley.

"Oh God, oh God," I cried out in pain.

Hell no, I told myself. *I'm not going to let these assholes see me suffer.*

So I hid the excruciating pain by pretending it was pure pleasure. But it was pure hell.

With six men penetrating me in every hole and way possibly imaginable, I became sicker and more twisted. When I became too weak to endure the pain, Satan himself entered me to give me unlimited strength. My green eyes became black and dilated. A hellish look on my face, I snarled into the camera.

Then the male pigs pulled out of me one by one and sprayed their liquid filth all over my red pointed face. A mouthful of bitter fluids and feces, I pretended to love every nauseating minute of it.

"Oh yeah baby, I love it," I lied through my tightly clenched teeth. The scene ended with the final guy who could barely squeeze out a drop. What a pig.

Someone threw me some Baby Wipes and told me what a good job I did. Wiping off the goo from my nose, mouth and eyes, the bitter taste from the male pigs stuck to the bottom of my throat.

Vodka, I thought. *I need Vodka now.*

I lifted myself to go to the bathroom but when I sat up the pain shot throughout my body. I grabbed a Baby Wipe and gently reached around to clean my red swollen ballooned ass.

Damn that hurt, I cursed.

Hobbling toward the shower, someone was using it.

Great, I thought. I'm the one with a face full of glop and some male pig beat me to the shower. I grabbed some more Baby Wipes and headed to the room where my bags were instead.

"That wasn't so bad after all, now was it, Roxy," said a male performer while I wiped the goo off my face.

"Go to hell," I told him.

That night I went home and smoked some weed and played the Ouija board to relax. When I asked my spirit guide what his name was, He spelled out:

J E S U S C H R I S T

XIII

★ LAST CHANCE: FINAL ACT ★

★ *Chapter Thirteen* ★

As the days grew deadlier and the nights grew darker, I knew something was very wrong with me. I went from performing in girl/girl scenes to performing in brutal rape scenes within months. Every minute was pure hell and yet, I thrived in the darkness. It had become my comforter, a hiding place for all of my ugliness. Six years of performing in strip clubs, I felt at ease in the dark. It also empowered me. A powerfully dark woman, I could slip into any character from victim to abuser. I could walk into a room as an angel of light or I could dominate a soul and torture it. I could pretend to be a glamorous porn star and love every minute of the abuse or act as the abuser and forcefully destroy my victims. Porn was the perfect place for me to act out my *diverse* abilities. Pornographers loved it. In fact, the darker I became, the richer pornographers became.

As I continued to make harder and grosser porn, I transformed from victim into abuser. In my professional life, I began to act out like a man and abuse women on camera. With a strapped on dildo, I did to women exactly what men had done to me. I even knew how to selfishly stroke myself like a man. All those years in prostitution watching male pigs paid off. The men in porn were even worse pigs, ejaculating themselves on any weak woman on any sacred place on her body. I acted out in revenge the very thing I hated: a male pig.

I also abused men any chance I was given. In my private life, I had several male slaves who took care of me. I never once paid my electric bill during the last few years of my sex career. My slaves took care of things like that. I didn't even pump my own gasoline. Everywhere I went I dominated men and told them what to do. It was as if, no man could say no to me.

In my professional life, I continued to war with men in front of the camera. Every movie I made became a combat zone and I was determined to conquer. I was relentless. I even demanded movies be made in my apartment where I could control the atmosphere. With the Ouija Board by my side, demons in every corner and inside of me, I had full reign over my victims. I thought I was in total control of the darkness. I was not.

Unfortunately, when no one was looking of course, I fell apart. Tormented by demons every night, I lay on my bed for hours and listened to their vulgar and hateful words. I was so tormented that whenever I went outside and there was a full moon, the face on the moon cursed me and told me it hated me. I thought it might have been the drugs and alcohol but when I asked people around me to tell me what they saw, they turned to me in fear and asked me if I had been playing with the Ouija Board again.

I opened up a demonic world I wasn't prepared for and Satan wanted my life for it.

I cried out to God over and over to save me from Satan and myself, but God didn't seem to answer. I couldn't understand why God would not rescue me. I never doubted God or who Jesus was the entire time I was in the sex industry. But I doubted God's love for me. How could God allow so many bad things to happen if He was a God of love?

Blinded by the lies of pornography and Satanism, I continued on into the darkness. We all did. A world of fraud and wooden nickels, we ignored the obvious: Glamorous porn stars were jaded drug addicts. Friendly pornographers were machines of cruelty. Sexy purple couches were discolored beds of disease. Bathrooms were stations of human filth. Nothing was sacred in porn. Everything was diseased, destroyed and damned.

We were children of wrath, gratifying our sin natures with no thought of consequences. Some of us died in our ignorance. Some of us were waiting to die.

And then it was my turn.

The clock struck 10 and I felt it. A tiny bump on my labia, I wondered what it could be. Of course I ignored it like I ignored everything else in my life. Ignorance is bliss in the porn industry.

I was with a married couple that night. They saw one of my movies and requested *time* with me: a private date with a porn star.

As I walked out of the bathroom and adjusted my panties to hide my newly discovered "bump", I requested the lights be dimmed. I really wasn't interested in frightening the young married couple who hired a prostitute for the *first* time. Nobody needed to know about my little "bump" but me.

A week later I was abruptly awakened by a stinging between my legs and a high fever. Rolling out of bed, my lower back hurt terribly.

What is wrong with me? I thought.

Still drunk from the night before, I sluggishly walked over to the bathroom where I looked into the mirror. In shock I stared at an image of me with cracked lips and red sores. I looked like a monster. As I swallowed back the shock, my throat stung. A closer look into the mirror, I opened my mouth to examine my sore throat and discovered a HUGE quarter sized red sore on the back of my throat.

"What is THAT??" I blurted out loud.

I pulled my lips back and red sores were everywhere in my mouth. I was horrified. I couldn't believe it. I didn't know what it was.

This is bad, I thought.

I peeled off my panties to look for possible further damage. Fluid-filled blisters were everywhere. I grabbed my hand held mirror to look from behind.

Oh my God, I thought.

Blisters were everywhere on my vagina and anus. I didn't dare touch myself lest they get on my hands. I stood up, mystified and in awe. Nothing like this had *ever* happened to me.

I threw on some clothes, jumped in the car and drove down to the nearest medical clinic. When it was finally my turn to be examined, the insensitive Indian doctor exclaimed, "Oh my, you have huppies."

"What the hell is huppies?" I demanded to know.

He explained to me I had a bad case of Genital Herpes, a non-curable disease, and took a sample of my blood for more testing. I was dumbfounded. I couldn't believe it. If I scared the doctor with my Herpes, it must be *really* bad.

Oh my God, I thought again. *I have an infectious non-curable disease.*

An evil laugh interrupted my shocking thoughts and a low voice spoke to me, "No one will love you now. You are nothing but an ugly monster. No one will want you. You might as well kill yourself."

Yeah, I nodded my head. *I should just kill myself.*

That day I drove home and took over 30 prescription pills. This time I was serious. My life was a wreck. I had nothing to live for. Everyone hated me. Nobody loved me. My parents didn't care. God didn't care.

Why should I care, I thought.

And I overdosed again, only this time I suffered through it alone in the darkness with a pack of demons by my bed crossing their fingers it would *finally* be over.

"Die, Shelley. Just die. We hate you. You are worthless. You're a piece of shit. Nobody wants you. God hates you. Just die!"

The evil voices hissed at me all night long.

But somehow I woke up. And then I disappeared. I quietly left the porn industry forever. I stopped taking calls. I stayed away from clubs and parties. I pretended like it never happened.

With no other options available to me, I went back to prostitution where I could at least use a condom. Nobody would have to know I had Herpes. That would remain my little secret. I called up old tricks and was on my way to work when a Voice interrupted my thoughts,

"Shelley, you're going the wrong direction."

I felt a very serious warning wash over me as I continued to drive on the 60 freeway heading west to Los Angeles.

"STOP!" the Voice boomed in my head.

Tears filled my eyes and I argued back, "God, I don't want to go back. I hate prostitution. But you're not helping me."

"STOP!" the Voice boomed again.

I couldn't shake the awful feeling that something very bad, something worse than what I could ever imagine was about to happen. I gulped down some Jack Daniels to ease my anxiety. I put in a cassette tape to drown out the Voice.

Everything will be okay, I reassured myself.

A sudden crash flipped my car up into the air and I saw the road flip upside down and around and around while I watched my life flash before my eyes.

"CRASH, BOOM!"

My car landed perfectly right side up. In shock, I grabbed the rear view mirror. No blood on my face. I looked down. No blood on my knees. I looked to the side. The car door was smashed in. I turned my head. The back window was shattered.

Everything was crushed except me. I didn't have a scratch.

I crawled out of my window and ran as fast as I could in shock. I looked behind me to see police lights driving up to the wreckage. I motioned to a driver to pull over and pick me up. I told him to take me home. He wanted to take me to the hospital. I told him my daughter was home alone and I had to get her.

I lied.

As we drove away, I watched the view in the mirror of black and white police cars pulling up to my crashed in red Miata convertible.

The only thought on my mind: I don't want to get a DUI.

I went home and called the police and lied that someone had stolen my car from a party. When I hung up the phone I just sat there in shock.

Maybe God was talking to me.

Oh yeah, I thought. *Between Herpes and a near fatal car accident, God is SO talking to me.*

A few days later I went down to the police impound to claim my crushed vehicle. I walked toward the red wreck in awe. The car was half the size it was before the accident. That's how crushed it was. I reached inside to grab some of my things and noticed the tape player still had the cassette I had popped in before the wreck.

98

It ejected out and I jumped back. The song that was playing during the accident was "Last Chance" by Duran Duran. I had no idea.

Gulp. God was definitely talking to me.

★ *Admit One* ★

★ **ACT IV** ★

★ *Two Worlds Collide* ★

XIV

★ *Admit One* ★

★ POOF, HE'S HERE! ★

★ *Chapter Fourteen* ★

I was so bored. I had no car. I couldn't drive anywhere and I was sick of asking sugar daddies to drive me around. They couldn't keep their hands off of me. I was so sick of men.

During my "off" time I pulled out my New Age books and practiced my psychic techniques. I figured God was trying to talk to me so I should try to go to the other side. At least that's what the "voice" told me.

I believed in Jesus and God and remembered when Jesus told me I was special. I was only six years old but I never forgot the vision I saw of me preaching to a crowd of thousands of people. Maybe there was still a chance? I mean, He did just save my life from a near fatal car accident.

I got *really* good at my powers. I practiced them all day long where I sat on the floor surrounded by white candles. I loved candles. Of course I did, I was a creature of the dark!

At first the voice seemed friendly and I was sure the Holy Spirit was talking to me. Even the Ouija Board told me my spirit guide was Jesus Christ. It also told me I was a Chosen One and had been given great healing powers. Of course my ego loved to hear how special I was.

From mind over matter to energy manipulation, I used my powers for everything. If I wanted the phone to ring, poof it rang. If I wanted a curtain to move, poof it moved. I was moving and manipulating things left and right. In fact, I even poofed my four year old daughter who fell over on the other side of the room! Everything in the psychic world came so easy to me. Of course, I was already a master manipulator.

After about six weeks of being locked up in a New Age world, I finally got my car back and wanted to mess with peoples' minds. I was also low on cash and needed to pull a few deals. I ended up at a bar in Covina where a couple of bands were playing.

Minding my own business at the bar someone tapped my shoulder. I turned around to a tall American apple pie looking guy who asked me if I wanted to play pool.

I coolly replied, "For drinks, sure."

I knew I could beat him. He obviously didn't know who he was messing with. He was just a little boy to me. He looked no older than 23.

Probably lived with his parents, I thought.

When he popped a quarter in and racked the balls tightly within a minute, I started to worry. This guy was no stranger to the pool table. The hustler in me quickly rose up. I didn't lose well and I certainly wasn't about to lose to *this* guy. That's when I started poofing.

"POOF!" I said while I aimed my hands at his pool stick. He looked at me like I was crazy, laughed and then made the shot perfectly. This guy wasn't even bothered by any of my poofs. I downed a shot of Bacardi and resorted to other means of manipulation: I pulled my top down. That's when he missed the shot.

We ended up downing Kamikaze shots -- on him, of course. That's when he asked me to play darts. Okay, darts was for nerds. But I was bored, he offered me free drinks and besides he was a nice guy. He didn't once talk to my boobs.

That was different.

As he was sharing his personal information, which I didn't listen to any of it, I noticed out of the corner of my eye that he was hitting the bull's-eye almost every time! This guy was a hustler or something. He intrigued me. But of course I wasn't interested in love or anything. I was interested in his skills and especially his wallet. Maybe behind this smart guy was a rich guy. A diseased prostitute could only dream.

Tall, blonde and not very handsome, he was only 22 years old and worked at a box plant. Okay, he doesn't have money. *Forget it,* I told myself.

"Hey, what's your number?" he asked me.

"Um, I don't date for free. I'm a stripper. Cash only." My eyes zeroed in on his pocket. He realized I was all about the money and so he lied and said he needed a stripper for a bachelor's party.

"Right," I told him. This little boy would probably pee his pants if he ever saw a naked woman, I snickered. I handed him my card just in case he *really* needed a stripper.

"Three hundred an hour, babe. See ya," and I walked out of his life forever.

A week later the phone rang.

God, I hope it's not someone from the porn industry, I worried.

I answered the phone in a fake English accent, "E-llo?"

"Hey um, Giovanni, you wanna play pool tonight?"

"Who is this?" I asked in an irritated English accent.

"This is Gary. We met at the bar a couple weeks ago."

Okay, I had to think about this one. Everywhere I went I met guys. I paused a second to try and remember. Okay, I gave up.

"No, I don't remember you." I went back to my regular voice.

"I'm the guy you played pool with at Boar's Head and shot darts with."

"Ohhh, okay I think I remember you. Um, well, it's Friday night. I have to work tonight."

"I have to work too," he said. "I just thought we could hang out a few hours before I go to work at ten."

"No, not tonight, but thanks." I hung up the phone. I didn't have time for little boys. I needed to make some money.

But the guy kept calling me! Over the next month I told him "no thanks" repeatedly and that I needed to work. I mean, he could have offered me money. I hinted enough.

Finally on another Friday night he called me again. This time I was sitting home alone tired of trying to figure out if I was officially back in prostitution or not. I hated stripping. I hated prostitution. Maybe this guy called me on the right night.

"Okay, I'll play pool with you but you buy the drinks," I told him bluntly. I figured I would at least get something out of it. Not to mention, maybe make some "deals" at the bar. I could pull a trick anywhere.

"Sure, see you soon!" He sounded like a giddy school boy.

What have I gotten myself into, I thought.

We met at the bar and the guy totally surprised me that night. Not only did he drive like a speed demon but at one of

106

the bars we stopped off at, he walked right up to the pool table and lined it with speed.

"Holy shit!" I exclaimed. "Where the hell did you get all of that meth?" I looked up at apple pie guy in shock.

"I always have it. You like to fly?"

Well, of course I like to fly, I thought. I missed my speed. The porn industry was my main drug supplier so it had been a little while.

Wow, I thought. This could be the beginning of a beautiful long lasting relationship.

If only I had known.

Gary started coming over with his meth. We snorted. We talked. We stayed up all night and laughed. He was really a nice guy. He never tried to make a single move on me.

A burned out prostitute could get used to this, I thought.

One night he brought over checkers.

"Um, what are the checkers for?" I said with a funny look.

"They're to play with, silly."

"Um, I don't play checkers." He laughed and set the game up. When he said he could beat me at any game, that's when he pushed the right button. I was extremely competitive not to mention a major control freak. *No one* dared me to a game and won. No one!

The creep beat me. I hated him. Of course I wanted to play again and again and again. No way could I let this guy win.

We played Gin Rummy, 5 Card Stud Poker, Texas Hold 'em, and more. We just played games. It had been years since I played games with anyone.

I still hadn't told Gary my past or even my horrible present. I was hoping we could just stay "game" friends for a while. But one night he came to my house and saw me signing an autographed picture for the security guards.

"What is that?" he asked.

"Well, um, I was a porn star."

"Oh, okay." He just walked into the house and set up checkers. That was weird.

I marched right into the house and blurted out, "Don't you know what kind of woman I am? I'm a hooker, a prostitute, a stripper and I worked in porno movies!"

Unaffected he asked me, "How did you get into stripping?" I couldn't believe it. Most men would have asked me to have sex by now. Not Gary. He really wanted to know what happened to me. So, I told him how I got kicked out of the house at 18 and ended up on the streets of the San Fernando Valley. I told him a pimp lured me in and offered me money when I was homeless. He was shocked, even appalled by my tragic story. His whole face changed and he reached his hand out to hold mine.

"Shelley, that's terrible what happened to you." I thought I was going to throw up.

Oh shit, I thought. *This guy actually cares about me.* I ripped my hand back.

Nervous, I quickly changed the subject and asked him how he got into drugs.

"Dad and Mom were pastors."

What? I thought. *Gary is a Pastor's kid?*

"Yeah, my dad cheated on my mom with the church secretary when I was 17. Our home was never the same. My dad became a sailor mouthed alcoholic and it drove my family apart. I started doing drugs when I was 20 years old."

"You've only been doing drugs for two years?"

"Yep."

Oh wow, I thought. This guy is ripe. I wondered if he still lived with Mommy and Daddy.

"Where do you live?" I asked.

"I live with my parents in Chino."

Oh shit, I was right, I thought. *He lives with his parents.*

I couldn't believe I let some innocent pastor boy into my life. How did I not see this? How did this get past me? I started to freak. The demons in me were *not* happy.

"Shelley, do you believe in God?"

Dang, he wants to talk about God. I had a terrible feeling I was being set up.

"Of course I believe in God. I was raised in Sunday School when I was a little girl." Something inside of me lit up because I spent the next fifteen minutes going on and on about God. It was probably the speed.

"And then I was in a church play called, 'Pilgrim's Progress' and I played Faithful, the pilgrim who is Christian's friend from the City of Destruction."

"Wow, I know that story. You played Faithful?" he asked.

"Yeah, and I even memorized the alphabet backwards when I sang the Z to A song. In fact, God told me when I was nine years old that the guy I would marry someday would be able to say the alphabet backwards as fast as I could."

Without hesitation he said:

"ZYXWVUTSRQPONMLKJIHGFEDCBA."

We both just stared at each other.

Furious, I stood up and told him to get out.

I never wanted to see him again. I ran upstairs to my bedroom and frantically stared into my reflection in the mirror for some answers.

Come on, Shelley, use your psychic abilities.

POOF, HE'S HERE!

★ *Admit One* ★

★ INVADED BY LOVE ★

★ *Chapter Fifteen* ★

Under no circumstances was I going to marry him. Years and years of buried pain protected by the rock-solid wall around my black heart; I was impenetrable.

I shoved the thought of Gary out of my mind and ran back to the lies and mental illness, the familiar dark world where I felt safe: a world without love and light. I turned off my phone and ripped the curtains closed. I would have nothing to do with him.

I went upstairs to take a shower to wash away whatever Gary had deposited into me. The stream of hot water on my face, tears poured out of my eyes. I missed him.

The low voice hissed at me, "We don't need him. Get him out of your mind. Remember your bottle of Jack Daniels behind the toilet?"

I grabbed the bottle and guzzled it down. The warm feeling washed over my body and I dried off and collapsed into bed. Shoving my face into the pillow, I cried myself to sleep.

"Mommy, are you okay?" a small voice woke me.

"Hey honey, Mommy just took a little nap. What do you want?" I said as I rubbed my eyes.

"There's a man at the door with a box."

"What??" I was irritated. It was probably one of my sugar daddies breaking the rules again. They knew better than to come over here without calling.

Idiots.

Half-drunk and angry, I headed downstairs and ripped open the door and shouted, "What are you doing here!"

The voice behind the box replied, "I brought you a box of rags. I came over to clean your house."

My mouth dropped open.

Gary walked right into my world and over to the table where he set down a box of neatly folded white towels. He looked up and smiled at me with a rag in his hand while I stood there and stared.

"Shelley, I feel bad for you. Your house is really messy. You need someone to take care of you."

Then he vanished around the corner and suddenly I heard water running.

I felt a terrible blow to my chest. Pain radiated up my spine through my neck to my face and jaws. I sat down on the couch and grabbed a cigarette out of the ashtray. Frantically trying to light it, I gasped the airy smoke into my lungs.

I can't do this, I thought as gray smoke blew out of me. Rocking back and forth on my couch with arms folded around me, a terrible feeling washed over me. I need air, I thought.

I walked outside on the porch looking around for anything that made sense. There was no comfort. There was no way out of this horrible pain. I couldn't breathe.

"Shelley, are you okay?" A figure out of the smoke came towards me.

It was Gary. I stepped back. I was desperately afraid of him.

"Stay there. I don't feel comfortable."

"Shelley, it's just me, it's Gary. I don't want to hurt you. Please..."

"No, back off." I scowled and threw my cigarette on the ground and stepped on it.

I ran upstairs to my bedroom and locked the door and hid beneath the bed sheets.

Shaking and frightened by the intense pain, I cried out to God, "God, take it away. Please God, take it away." The voices started yelling at me:

Stupid whore. No one will ever love you. He will use you and hurt you just like everyone else did. Get away from him!

Another Voice interrupted, "Shelley, be still and know Me. Gary has been sent by Me to help you. It's time."

"Time? For what?" I asked the Voice. I waited for an answer but it was silent. Even the other voices were gone now.

I sat up and stared in the mirror at the ugly woman looking back at me. Blonde hair extensions sticking out of my dark roots with dark circles under my eyes, I was a horrible wreck. How could Gary even want to be near such a mess?

He would leave me, I just knew it. I had to protect myself. I put on my false front face and acted like I didn't care. I went downstairs to end the whole thing.

"Gary, I..."

He turned around with the most angelic smile and a perfect shiny kitchen behind him.

"Yes?"

I was speechless. My heart melted and the evil within me recoiled. He walked toward me, touched my face and kissed me softly. A spongy warm sluggish kiss, I wanted to eat his lips. I hadn't been softly kissed by a man in years.

Our beautiful kiss ended and I buried my head in his chest and wept bitterly. Huge tears of shattered years gushed out of my eyes and the forceful pain of Rejection, Rage and Hatred rose up from deep within. I violently pushed him away and pulled out my hair.

"I hate you!!! I hate them!!!" I grabbed the phone and threw it. I threw the trash can. I punched the couch. I spit. I hit. I kicked. I hated them!

"I hate them! I hate men! I hate all of you! Go to hell f—kin' losers!" I threw my seashell across the room. Gary was shocked but held his ground.

"Stay the f—k away from me! F—k you!" I screamed violently at him. The evil inside of me was so fuming mad and all hell broke loose inside of me.

"F—k you, loser. You liar. I hate you. Get away from me!"

I grabbed a knife in the kitchen and fiercely aimed it at him. Pointing at him full of rage, I told him to get the hell out and stay out forever.

"Get the hell away from me, NOW!" Wild strands of bleached hair in my face, I panted like a ferocious animal.

"Shelley, I love you. I love you. I love you. I'm not giving up on you."

The knife slipped out of my hand.

My body fell to the floor and I wept.

His overwhelming love crucified me. It shredded the very core of every deception I held dear and did the unthinkable: it gave me hope. For the first time in over seventeen years I felt hope in my heart.

A massive wreck on the floor, Gary held me close in his arms and wholeheartedly prayed.

"Lord, I ask you to heal Shelley; to heal every wound from the top of her head to the soles of her feet. I know you can do it, Jesus. In your name I pray, amen."

It was the prayer that changed my life forever.

The one that God heard and hell listened to.

And the war for my life began.

XVI

★ *Admit One* ★

★ MARRYING MAGDALENE ★

★ *Chapter Sixteen* ★

A heart-shaped ring, I said yes. I wasn't attracted to him. I didn't really love him. But he loved me. That was what mattered. Besides, where else would I find a guy who wanted to marry a washed up porn star with Herpes and a kid?

"Shelley, please marry me. God sent me to you."

Does God know I'm a bitch?

We drove to Norwalk, California, on a harsh winter's day on February 14th, 1995. There was no white wedding, only a cloudy gray one. The cold steps of the court house were every little girl's nightmare. I especially thought the homeless guy would have made a good flower girl.

As usual, I was in a bad mood that day.

"Are you sure we don't have to have an appointment? It's probably too busy today." I tried to think of ways to get out of it. Reality hit me after that first kiss and I realized this was *never* going to work.

"No, we don't have to have an appointment. It's the Valentine's Day Special today. They're offering marriages all day."

Great, the Valentine's Special. Gee, what a lucky girl I am, I sarcastically thought.

Dressed in a torn black floral dress, I looked like I was going to a funeral. *Yeah, my funeral,* I thought.

We stood in line and then it was our turn.

"Hello, may I please see your photo I.D.s?" the lady behind the cracked window asked.

"Sure," I said unenthusiastically as I handed her our I.D.s and the application. I was the one in charge of course.

"How much for a marriage license?" I asked smugly with a look of disgust on my face.

"That'll be thirty-five dollars please."

I choked on my spit.

"Wait, how much did you say?"

"That'll be thirty-five dollars please."

Damn, I thought. That's how much I got paid for my first trick!

Then a Voice spoke to my heart, "Thirty-five dollars to get into the sex industry and thirty-five dollars to get out."

Only God could have known that.

I lowered my head and looked down at my tattered shoes. Could God really be rescuing me? I was so dirty and unworthy.

Gary took my hand and led me upstairs to a bright white hall where other couples waited against the wall for their number to be called. I stopped and stared at the wall contemplating the huge life decision before me. Evil voices tried to talk me out of it. Gary saw my struggle and squeezed my hand harder and said, "You can do this, Shelley."

"I can't do this, Gary. I can't." I cringed under my breath and turned my pale face into the white wall. Gary put his arms around me from behind and whispered gently, "You can do this, Shelley. God is with us."

The voices in my head argued, *"You're too sick. He will leave you. He doesn't know how sick you are. When he finds out about you, he will leave you. Hurry, run now!*

A terrible sick feeling washed over me and I felt like throwing up. The voices were right. Gary didn't know what he was marrying. He didn't know about my sick and twisted sexual abuse. He didn't know how bad my addictions were. He didn't know I was a manipulator and liar. He didn't *really* know me. He had no understanding of the powerful hold Satan had on my life. It was a war he wasn't ready for.

"Gary, we can't do this. It's not fair to you. I am not who you think I am. I am much worse. I have so many demons. I will hurt you."

"Shelley, you can never hurt me. I love you. God is with us."

"I can't," I insisted as I tugged on his shirt and lowered my face into his chest.

A voice came out of the room, "Number 15."

They called our number. I looked up at Gary with fear in my eyes. If he wouldn't listen to me at least I wanted him to see the terror in my eyes.

He held my hand securely and walked me over to a black woman wearing a black gown. It was a sign, I knew it. I looked up at him in fear again. His gentle blue eyes smiled back at me.

We repeated our vows or should I say Gary did. I was frozen in shock. All I remember is saying, "I will." I will? I didn't have a will. I only had death and destruction.

We walked out of the white building into dark clouds and pouring rain. Gary interrupted the storm and asked me if I wanted a hamburger at Wendy's next door. I shook my head no in disgust. I didn't eat meat anyway.

The mental illness rose up in me and I repulsed Gary with my bizarre request to hurry up and consummate the marriage. It was the ritualist in me. He told me to please wait until he got back home from work. He wanted to take me out to a romantic dinner and celebrate. I wanted cold hard unfeeling sex. I wanted to hate him right away.

I got what I wanted. After we finished I pushed him off of me and told him I wanted a divorce.

"Get away from me! I want a divorce! I hate you. You're nothing but a male pig!"

Pain and Abuse reared their ugly heads and threatened to throw something at him. He immediately put on his clothes and left. His face was so hurt. I knew I had hurt him. Good, I hated men.

The evil in me was satisfied and we celebrated yet another failure in my life with our favorite bottle of relief: Jack Daniels.

He would have left me anyway, I tried to reassure myself with splashes of Jack down my throat. But why did I have an awful feeling that I just lost the most important thing in my life? I felt sick. I wanted to throw up.

Oh God, I thought. *What have I done?*

I wanted to die. The emotional toll was too much for me and I downed most of the bottle of Jack. I laid on the floor holding and stroking my bottle. He was my only trusted friend, Jack. Drunk, I fell asleep.

"Shelley, Shelley, wake up." I opened my eyes to a beautiful bouquet of red roses with a big white bow hanging in my face.

"Huh?" I tried to sit up.

"I love you. Happy Wedding Day, honey," Gary said as he bent down and kissed my Jack Daniels filled mouth. I felt so gross and unworthy.

I sluggishly thanked him and told him I didn't want to go out to dinner. I felt horrible for my awful behavior and tearfully apologized. He brushed my hair to the side and kissed my cheek.

"It's okay, honey. I know you're hurting badly. I'm here for you."

I buried my head in his strong chest and I wailed. No one had ever loved me in my life like Gary did. No one. I never had a mother's love. I never had a father's love. I only knew pain and abuse since I was a small child. I dug my fingernails deep into his skin and squeezed him with every ounce of pain I had inside of me. He was my giant Cross, someone who could take my pain and let me nail it on him.

And I nailed it hard. I pounded him with every powerful lie, expressions of rage and hatred, vulgarities and evil fits and he took it. He took the excruciating pain for me.

He became Christ to me and I became his penitent whore, like the sinful woman with seven demons. Only I had more than seven. I had *legions*.

Black dilated eyes and an evil smile against his chest, let the exorcism begin.

XVII

★ YOU AND WHAT ARMY? ★

★ *Chapter Seventeen* ★

The next few months were pure hell. Gary lost his job and had to have knee surgery. His mother tried to make him divorce me. His aunt called child protective services to try and get Tiffany taken away from us and his dad left his mom right after we got married. What are the odds?

The devil wasn't going to let me get away that easily.

I wanted a divorce. Gary wanted to fight for us. So, he put down the meth and joined the United States Army.

Army, I thought. *I loved military men.*

"When do we leave?" I asked.

"We don't leave. I do," he answered back.

"Excuse me?"

"Shelley, I have to go to Basic Training for ten weeks in South Carolina and then I have to do advanced training in San Antonio, Texas for another eight weeks. But after that we can be together."

What the hell was I going to do? I thought.

I'll tell you what I did. I did what any psychopath, ex sex worker wife would do; I went to a psychiatrist and got a doctor's note. It was the only way to get the Army to let me come along during his training. Yes, I manipulated the United States Army.

Gary wasn't happy about my stunt at all. It must have been terrible when his Commander called him to the office to tell him the Red Cross had an emergency message from his mentally ill wife and that she needed him to come home and move her to Texas. Gary had to redo his entire schooling because of my little stunt.

Well, I *was* mentally ill. It's not like I lied or anything. I just, sort of, used it.

Gary looked *so* good when I saw him. I couldn't believe it. Two grueling months of the Army's basic training program, Gary looked incredible! He also came back with a powerful new name: Private Garrett Lubben. The Army didn't allow nicknames. The military had made a real man out of him!

Garrett, I could get used to that, I thought.

There was just one problem. Garrett was sober and all healed up. I was a cesspool of mental disorders, addiction and demonic strongholds. Not only that, Garrett had a new beautiful physique while I rapidly gained weight in recovery. I felt uglier and more unworthy than ever before.

"There's just more of you to love, Shelley."

Gee, thanks for noticing my fat. Well, at least I couldn't go back to the sex industry. No one would hire me now.

When we got to Texas I had to find a job. The military paid Garrett almost nothing and so the first day we arrived at Fort Sam Houston, I hiked down the street to the Sunset Lounge and got a job as a bartender.

Finally, I was on the other end of the bar. I was a pro. Of course I was, I was a raging alcoholic. There was no drink I couldn't concoct and customers loved me. We partied all day and night while Garrett suffered through intense military training. I only saw him every other weekend. Tiffany stayed with a babysitter in our new apartment building. Things started looking up and I felt like I had a new leash on life.

Unfortunately, the collar quickly fell off and I made a huge terrible mistake. One night when I was drunk and the cash was low, I foolishly agreed to have sex for money. In my inebriated messed up mind, I was trying to help support my family. I was also addicted to fast easy money.

Demons and alcohol tried to destroy my life once again. I found out three weeks later I was pregnant and I literally went through the roof. The man I had sex with was black. Garrett was going to kill me for sure. I hated myself and wanted to die.

The night I had sex with the man, I felt so guilty. I knew it was wrong. Prostitution didn't come easy to me anymore. I felt horrible so I only had sex for about a minute with a condom and then pushed him away because I knew it was wrong. I couldn't go through with it and yet, here I was pregnant.

I was a cursed woman. I had to tell Garrett the truth. I stupidly called him on the phone.

"Garrett, I have some terrible news. Do you promise not to leave me?"

"Yes, Shelley, I promise."

"I had sex with someone else when I was drunk..."

Garrett didn't say a word.

"...and now I'm pregnant."

The phone hung up.

125

I really screwed it up this time, I thought. I got into the bathtub, turned on the water and sobbed giant tears of regret. I was the most sorry I had ever been in my life. I hated what I had done. I hated my sin against Garrett and against God. How could I have let this happen?

I desperately begged God, "Please God, please God, let this baby be Garrett's. Please forgive me and have mercy on me. I promise to obey you. I promise!"

Garrett came home that weekend and didn't say a word. I followed him around begging him for forgiveness swearing to God I would do whatever it took to save our marriage. I even promised to stop drinking.

I also promised him that when the baby was born if it wasn't his I would give it up for adoption. He agreed to stand by me no matter what. But I saw the pain in his eyes. I crushed his big beautiful heart.

Garrett finally finished his schooling and received orders to go to Fort Lewis, Washington. *Thank God,* I thought. I had to get out of Texas and away from that bar!

We drove all the way across country in a little black Datsun truck I bartered from one of my bar customers. Poor Tiffany had to sit behind my seat for two thousand miles. Good thing a cop didn't pull us over.

After a sober drive along the Oregon Coast, I heard a Voice say within, *"Trust me, Shelley."*

I had no choice but to trust God. I had no one else to lean on. Garrett was gone all the time and barely talked to me when he was home. My parents weren't around and didn't care much. My mother in law couldn't stand me. I had no friends to talk to. It was just me and God and the little baby growing inside of me.

"Baby, I am sorry your mommy is so stupid. I really love you." I looked down in tears at my little bump. My heart broke at the thought of having to give my baby up. Every day I got down on my knees and begged God to have mercy and please let the baby be Garrett's.

"Please God, have mercy on me. You saved me all those times during the sex industry. Save me one more time, please." I wept and wept. I was deeply sorry for my sins.

I was an emotional wreck. I began to experience regular flashbacks and nightmares of my horrible past. Images of foul men penetrating me in every orifice haunted me every night. I woke up screaming and punching my pillow. During the day I lived through constant mood swings. One minute I was angry and throwing things and the next I was on the floor sobbing in tears. Garrett thought it was pregnancy hormones. But I knew it was more than that. I was battling real demons and I needed real help.

I knew I needed to go to church. Desperate for any help I could get, I pulled out the Yellow Pages and chose the first church I landed my finger on.

"Champion's Centre," sounded good enough to me.

Sunday came and we pulled up to a glamorous big church in our ugly beat up Datsun. I was so embarrassed. Everybody looked happy and shiny; moms and dads with happy little children running around. It made me cringe. I hated the family I grew up in.

As soon as I walked in I experienced massive culture shock. The music was earsplitting and people were jumping up and down waving their hands in the air.

Why the hell were these people so happy, I wondered.

"ALL THINGS ARE PO-SS-I-BLE," sang and danced a thunderous choir of purple robed people.

Struck by the bright lights and powerful music around me, I fell into a chair in the crowd and lowered my head. Paranoid, I thought someone might know me. I looked over at Garrett and his face was lit up like a kid at a carnival. He was used to the light and the music. I was used to death and darkness. I just sat there and stared.

The music stopped and some young guy walked onstage praising the Lord.

"Success begins on Sunday!" the pastor exploded. Then he opened a book and said he was teaching on the nine tests that prove some kind of potential or something like that. None of it made sense to me. I was about to get up when he stopped and pointed his finger directly at me.

"Do you know there's a Champion inside of you?"

The truth hit my face like a half-ton truck.

Kicking and screaming inside of my soul, the talented Champion little girl in me was *dying* to get out. She had been locked up in a hell cell for over seventeen years and she wanted out!

Overwhelmed by the powerful words of the Pastor, I burst into violent tears and seventeen years of pent up pain exploded out of me. I began to mourn for my shattered life. A blob of a million traumatized pieces, I wailed over the injustices done against me since I was a child. I screamed out in pain at the utter wickedness of my parents' betrayal. I sobbed over the self-hatred against my own soul. I utterly hated myself.

The entire service became my funeral and evil lie after lie was exposed. It was the truth encounter of a lifetime and it was only the beginning.

The eulogy of the dead, my unexpected funeral ended with me wiping my tears and the concluding pastor's words:

"Resist the devil and he will flee from you."

I knew right then what I had to do.

I went straight home, got down on my knees and prayed.

"Jesus, please forgive me for all of my sins, which are many. Please have mercy and help me get through this pregnancy. Please let this baby be Garrett's. Please, Lord. I know I deserve to be thrown out on the street or worse but Lord, I desperately need you."

As I was praying, someone entered my front room. I recognized the Presence right away. It was Jesus. The same Jesus I knew as a little girl and the same Jesus that was with me on the porn set. He never left my side for a moment. I repented for every sin I ever committed and utterly thanked Him that I wasn't burning in hell.

Someone else entered the room. A dark intimidating presence, I recognized the familiar evil force. But the Lord wasn't moved. Strong and beautiful, He stretched out His hand and dared me to do the impossible.

Bible in my hand, baby in my tummy and newborn faith, I reached up to Jesus and together, we declared war on Satan.

My beautiful mother and I   A four year old happy little girl.
on my first birthday.

Me singing my heart out to Jesus!

Me as a poppy in a play.   *Aw, aren't I an angel at 8?*

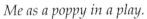

Sweet

 Me in my front yard in Glendora. The big orange grove behind me was perfect for orange fights!

Me on halloween dressed up as a sexy witch!

Me and my Miss Piggy Puppet. I could imitate her and still can!

I REALLY loved Miss Piggy and rollerskating, too!

Twelve years old and hated my glasses! But loved my hair.

Me at 15 years old with dreams of being a Hollywood actress.

A playboy bunny for halloween at 14.

Me in 9th grade in drill team.

134

Me barely graduating Glendora High School in 1986.

La Huera Loca

Blondie
1987-1992

Giovanni

Marilyn

1-800-Prostitute

136

Liar. *Hater.* *Whore.*

Porn destroyed my life from 1993-1994

The New Shelley

Shelley in 2008

Shelley in 2009

Jennifer Williams

Me with my Healing Bible the
day before I testified in
California State Legislature.

Me on the Lexi Show sharing the Gospel and telling the shocking truth about pornography.

Me speaking at the June 15 briefing to the U. S. Congress

Heather, Patrice, Julie, Shelley, Jan, Vicky, and Tammy.
Ex porn stars and ex strippers at Adult Entertainment Expo 2009

140

Bryan Hall

Abigail, Teresa, Tiffany, Mommy and Daddy in 2006

Lubben Family decked out in Pink Cross shirts in 2009

Jennifer Williams

141

Shelley and Garrett Lubben's 15th Anniversary on Valentine's Day 2010

★ *Admit One* ★

★ **ACT V** ★

★ *Meet Shelley #2* ★

XVIIII

★ *Admit One* ★

★ **THIS IS ONLY A TEST** ★

★ *Chapter Eighteen* ★

Blessed is the man who perseveres under trial, because when he has stood the test, he will receive the crown of life that God has promised to those who love him.

- James 1:12

Front and center, I was in that church every Wednesday and Sunday. Garrett was slaving away for the military while I was learning how to pass tests to prove my personal potential. Three months pregnant with a baby and hope for the future, I began my days with prayer and a flip through the Bible. At night I worked at the Acapulco Mexican restaurant as a food server.

From La Huera Loca to a humble Mexican waitress, I joyfully welcomed customers at the door,

"Bienvenidos a Acapulco restaurante."

When I spoke Spanish, my Mexican boss asked me where I learned it.

"I'm from California," I half smiled back.

Sundays were my favorite day of the week. I loved to shove my way into church to get the best seat. It was all about me at that point.

"The goal for every achiever is to pass the test," the pastor preached. As he went down the list of nine tests to prove one's personal potential, I failed them all.

"Are you easily offended?" he asked.

"No!"

"What about the motivation test, why do you do what you do?" the pastor asked the congregation.

Because I want something, duh.

"Do you have patience? Can you pass the test of time? Do you think long term?"

I wish he'd hurry up, I'm hungry. My pregnant tummy rumbled.

"Do you have respect for the authority God has placed in your life?"

Nobody tells me what to do, I thought with a smirk.

"How do others view you? Can you pass the credibility test?"

Gulp. I hated to think of how others viewed me. I'm pretty sure past sugar daddies could comment about that one. Years of using and abusing men entered my mind.

The pastor interrupted my thoughts. "You will be blessed in the city and blessed in the country. The fruit of your womb will be blessed…"

Okay, that one was for me, I thought. I looked down at my stuffed womb and made a tiny deal with God.

"I promise to obey you. Just please make this baby be Garrett's."

The service ended and it was time to go home and eat. I was starving!

I grabbed my daughter Tiffany from Sunday School and headed home for some Italian cuisine: macaroni and cheese. Yeah, it was gross but I couldn't afford "special" foods anymore and I didn't know how to cook. Tiffany liked it anyway.

Wet and rainy Washington weeks went by and it was time for my first pregnancy exam. I hadn't been to a doctor in years, except for the occasional overdose. That didn't really count though. This time it was special. I hoped they would let me hear the baby's heartbeat.

"Shelley Lubben," the name still sounded funny. A lifeless lady handed me a bunch of papers and told me to fill them out. Overwhelmed by the amount of questions they asked, I gasped out loud. The experienced military Mom sitting next to me chuckled and welcomed me to the Army life of "overkill of the paper trail".

Whatever that meant, I thought.

I slowly read over each question one by one.

No heart disease. No kidney disease. No blood disease. No HIV.

I hoped.

No liver disease, gulp.

I hoped again.

I felt so stressed out from my past. I just wanted to forget it and the stupid questions were nothing but a horrible reminder. The evil voices chimed in, *You'll never get over your past, whore.*

"Get out of here in Jesus name!" I commanded the devil under my breath. I stacked the papers back under the clip and dumped them off at the front desk. I couldn't answer all the questions. Maybe they wouldn't notice.

Almost an hour later they called my name.

Finally, I thought. *This place was slower than my grandmother.*

I took a pee test, entered the military exam room and laid there with my chunky legs stuck up in stirrups. I felt so humiliated, which was pretty weird for someone who "did it all" on camera. I tried to think of something else. The door opened and a lady in a white lab coat with no makeup walked in.

"Hello, I'm doctor so-and-so and I'll be giving you a physical exam as well as asking you a few questions. I notice you didn't fill out some of your paperwork. I'll need to know some of the answers today."

"Okay," I moaned.

After a wide-eyed exam and a mildly painful check up, the doctor told me she thought I was about four months pregnant. Yep, just what I thought.

Great, I really do need a miracle, I thought.

Then she brought up questions about my past. I tried to hide my shame by looking away. The last thing I wanted to do was talk about my past. But the doctor said it was important for the health of my baby. Sure, pull the mother strings, lady.

"Have you had any sexually transmitted diseases?"

Breathe, I thought.

Full of unprecedented shame I answered a low, "yes."

She clicked on her pen and began to write.

"Which ones?" She stared into my face with a blank military look.

"Herpes."

"Did you have them vaginally or just orally?"

"Both."

She continued to scribble.

Wait, why was she still writing? I worried.

After a couple of minutes she asked me if I was interested in being in a military study for pregnant women with Herpes. I started to breathe again and figured what the heck, what did I have to lose?

The businesswoman in me perked up. "What do I get?" I asked.

"We don't pay you but you will be given ultrasounds and special attention if you participate in the study."

The attention whore in me sat up and smiled.

"Okay, I'll be part of your study."

"We'll need to take some blood today and we'll also test you for HIV," the doctor pronounced.

Gulp. There was that three-letter catchword from hell. As if I didn't hear enough of it in the porn industry. HIV was the F-bomb of porn.

The exam ended and I grabbed my purse and headed out the door. The stress made me hungry so I stopped off at the local hamburger place and got the $1 buck burger special. I was on a new cheap seafood diet. Everything I saw for a buck I ate.

I was getting fatter. Garrett came home after weeks of being in the field and saw my flabby fat folds. I think I traumatized him. I felt so embarrassed. Between Herpes tests, staying sober and having an anonymous baby, it was just too much for a newly reformed ex porn star mom to stomach. So I ate.

And I read the Bible. And I watched Christian television. And I listened to the Pastor's tapes after he preached. I *really* tried to obey God in everything I did, but it was much harder than I realized. Passing the Champion tests on a military base full of men and alcohol *was going to kill me,* I thought!

Especially when I heard, *"When my grandma was ninety-two, she did PT better than you,"* beautiful male voices sang in cadence as I stared at their perfect physiques while I munched on a bag of Fritos.

Delicious, I thought. Of course, I meant the chips!

Sobriety was painful to say the least.

I really need a break, God, I thought.

It was Sunday again and I greedily grabbed a seat close to the front. With a pen and Bible in my hand, I scribbled hurried notes on my bulletin as I tried to keep up with the Pastor.

"...my people are destroyed for lack of knowledge."

No wonder my life sucked, I thought. No one ever really took the time to teach me anything. The Pastor continued the lesson. "People blame their lack of success on problems that they face. If they could only realize those problems are their opportunities to prove themselves."

Wow, I thought. A giant light went off inside of me. I *never* viewed my problems as opportunities. Then another light went off.

Wait, I thought. *If I had a bunch of big problems that would mean I actually had a lot of huge opportunities.*

Dang, I thought. *This guy's good.*

Service ended and I drove home thinking about ways I could face my problems as opportunities to prove myself. I remembered the Pastor's words, "Practice God's principles on purpose" and that I didn't have to be perfect. That was a relief! I also thought about that knowledge thing he said, "My people perish for lack of knowledge."

I didn't want to perish anymore. I was done with being a loser in life. I woke up Monday morning and drove to the nearest public library. When I walked through the doors I felt a huge breath of air come into my soul. The curious little girl in me was alive and she was excited to learn!

I eagerly grabbed books about *everything*. From cooking to pregnancy to types of plants in Washington State, I wanted to learn about everything around me. The smell of the books soothed my irritated mind. But when I got to the breastfeeding section I stopped. It was too painful to "hope" for such a special joy when I wasn't sure I was going to keep my baby. I plopped down in the aisle and lowered my awful head. I deeply yearned to keep my baby. Tears filled my eyes.

"Shelley, trust me. Get the book," a gentle Voice said.

I cried. It was *so* hard to trust God. I had been through so much pain and trauma from my past. It was so hard to trust. I didn't trust anyone. But I knew I had to trust God.

"Okay," I answered. I got the book.

Then it happened. I started cooking! Garrett was traumatized again. He came home to a full meal with garlic bread and everything. Yeah, I made spaghetti. I'm a WOP, remember? Italian cooking came natural to me. I remembered when my Italian grandmother taught me how to make Veal Scaloppini as a child. She gave me some of my best memories as a child. I wanted to be just like her. So, I made spaghetti and meatballs and my hungry husband and daughter Tiffany gobbled it down. My first meal was more like the Last Supper: Holy and heartily enjoyed!

Not long after that first cooked meal, the phone rang.

"Shelley, we need you to come into the medical clinic and see the doctor," a voice on the other end of the phone told me.

"Why, is the baby okay?" She sounded serious so it really concerned me.

"Please come down to the clinic and the doctor will speak with you."

I showed up at the clinic with big worried eyes but an even bigger trust in God. I told Him I really wasn't up for any bad news. I sat down and waited.

"Hurry up and wait," a military mom mumbled to me.

I waited and I waited and I waited. Finally, they called my name, "Shelley Lubben."

I rushed to the bathroom to take the perpetual pee test and hurried to the exam room. The doctor came in immediately and unemotionally said, "Shelley, we regret to inform you that you cannot be in our study for Herpes. You don't have Herpes."

I shook my head. "That's impossible. I was diagnosed with Herpes and was on Zovirax," I retorted.

151

"No, you do not have the Herpes Simplex Virus," the doctor unequivocally stated. Then she explained that the military offered advanced testing and that Madigan Army Medical Center, where I was tested, was one of the top medical centers in the Army and that the United States Army wasn't wrong.

I SAT THERE STUNNED.

Then she examined me while I laid there with glazed donut holed eyes. When she finished and left, I attempted to put my clothes on backwards. Then I heard an alien Voice from outer space say, "Shelley, I just threw that in extra for following Me."

"WHAT?"

I couldn't believe it. God healed me from Herpes simply for following Him. I hadn't even gotten good at the Champion principles yet. I barely passed a few tests and now suddenly I'm healed from a non-curable disease? I thought I was going to pass out half-naked. Overwhelmed with joy and complete shock, I stumbled my way to the car and swerved home. Only this time I wasn't hungry. I couldn't eat. Are you kidding?

GOD HEALED ME FROM HERPES!!!

Garrett came home and I wrapped my arms around him and smacked a big one on him.

"Guess what, baby?!" A huge smile flashed across my face.

"What is it, Shelley?"

I did my famous black preacher dance around the room and then I jumped up in his face and yelled, "I'M HEALED FROM HERPES! THE DOCTOR SAID MY TEST CAME BACK NEGATIVE AND I CAN'T BE IN THE STUDY!"

Garrett of course wanted to know all the details. I told him. We rejoiced. Then I dragged him into the bedroom and enjoyed my new Herpes-free marital status!

Those first few crazy months I'll never forget. God tested me with everything from the offense test to the Herpes test, the test of small things to a Washington State driver's license test, the HIV test to the credibility test.

Did I also mention the food handler's test? Oh yeah, I was thoroughly tested and you know what?

I PASSED!

★ SPECIAL MILITARY DELIVERY ★

★ *Chapter Nineteen* ★

"Because he has loved Me, therefore I will deliver him; I will set him securely on high, because he has known My name."
- Psalms 91:14 (NASB)

You can have my Bible when you pry it from my "paranoid, mentally disturbed, physically-abusive, cold, dead hand." I was just as determined as the next soldier to conquer my enemy. Nothing would stop me from proving myself to God and delivering a beautiful healthy *Dutch* baby.

Then I got the news at seven months pregnant.

155

"Ma'am, your baby is small. We need to run some tests and do an ultrasound."

Where are the bedside manners around here? I shook my head as I stared into their blank cold faces.

No wonder they're called grunts, I thought.

Garrett and I followed the nurse into the ultrasound room where yet *another* doctor came in to examine me. In an advanced medical center where secret bio weapons were rumored to be tested, I never had the same doctor. I started to feel like a human experiment.

"Your baby is playing hide and seek," the doctor said with a smile. Finally, a sign of life!

"Can you tell if it's a boy or girl?" I hoped it was a boy but of course I would love it if it was a girl.

"Your baby's foot is in the way." The doctor tried to move my baby around with her probe but because it was breech and stubborn, she couldn't do it. After twenty minutes she gave up and told me to go back in the exam room where we could talk.

Now what? I thought.

"Your baby is breech and is abnormally small due to uterine retardation. We'll probably have to do a C-section but not for another six weeks."

"My baby's retarded?!" I sprang up instantly.

"No, your baby is not retarded," the doctor tried to reassure me. "Your baby is not growing properly due to placental insufficiency and that's why he or she is small. It's called Intrauterine Retardation Growth and we will need to monitor your baby closely."

I started to cry. I blamed myself.

How could this happen? I thought. I was doing so well. I prayed and practiced God's Word and did everything the Pastor taught me. Now my baby was retarded.

I started to hyperventilate.

Garrett tried to calm me down. He felt really bad for me. He saw I was going through hell and then for me to receive a bad report about my baby, he knew it was too much.

"Honey," he said softly, "the baby is not retarded. The baby is just small for its gestational size and the doctor says they will monitor everything closely. Don't worry. God didn't bring you this far not to deliver a healthy baby."

I melted into his arms.

"And Shelley," he lifted my chin up and looked at me with his blue eyes, "I want you to know that I trust God that this baby is ours."

My heart died and I cried my eyes out. I desperately needed to hear those words. His big arms wrapped tightly around me, his right hand held my head while I wept on his chest. I missed my best friend so much. With him being gone all the time it was hard for us to become close again.

Maybe this painful moment happened for a reason, I thought.

Emotionally and physically worn out from recovery, work, pregnancy and bad news, the tapping of rain drops lulled me into a deep sleep while Garrett drove us home. One hundred fifty depressing rainy days a year, Seattle was known as the suicide capital of America; perfect for a recovering porn star.

A dark and dreary early morning, the moment of truth finally arrived on January 3, 1997, and I was ready to achieve the impossible. Bible in my bag, Garrett by my side and Jesus tucked in my heart, I boldly walked into the hospital prepared for whatever lay ahead.

Stripped down to nothing and ready for delivery, the nurses rolled me into a bright white operating room. Garrett, a man of great integrity and supernatural kindness, sat down next to me and gently held my nervous hand in his. He smiled at me and told me he would be there for me no matter what. I squeezed his hand back as I tried to sniff up the tears.

Please let this baby be Garrett's, I silently prayed to God.

Suddenly everything moved quickly. Quick and hushed talking, the doctors moved swiftly as they forcefully tugged and pulled on my numb abdomen. I began to worry if the anesthesia was still working as I repeatedly whispered names of Jesus under my breath.

When I saw Garrett, a trained combat medic, stand up to get a closer look, I knew the time was near. Eyes closed shut and heart set on the powerful truth of God's Word, *"You can do all things through Him who strengthens you,"* I laid there wrapped up in the greatest faith moment of my life when out of the blue three awe-inspiring words gushed out of Garrett's mouth:

"SHE'S SO WHITE!!!" Then he whipped his head around to look at me with a beaming smile.

"Oh my gosh, it's a girl?"

Huge tears of relief exploded out of my eyes. My God came through for me. The greatest Promise Keeper of my life, I utterly thanked Him over and over for the greatest miracle in my life.

"Thank you, Jesus. Thank you thank you thank you Lord," were the only words that burst forth from my mouth for about ten minutes. The nurses had never seen a more grateful mother.

After the military doctors took painstaking measures to check every crevice of my new baby, a sweet nurse handed me my soft beautiful daughter. I fell in love with my white powdery baby immediately.

"Why is she full of white powder?" I asked the nurse. I thought maybe they doused her in Baby Powder to give me an extra special "military" delivery.

"Oh that's just Vernix, honey, the white cheesy stuff that protects your baby's skin. Your baby was born early so she has extra."

Then I looked up into a heavenly corner in my room and sensed God chuckling. Apparently He was loving *and* hilarious.

Thus began a long intimate relationship with God, a true Father, and not some mean guy up in the sky with a hammer.

But a caring Father who loved me and had a powerful plan for my life.

As I lovingly held my newborn daughter Teresa I realized God loved me like I loved my new baby.

Amazing.

XX

★ MAMA'S HEART TRAUMA ★

★ *Chapter Twenty* ★

Surely he has borne our griefs and carried our sorrow.
- Isaiah 53:4 (NASB)

God became my Father. He knew how much I would need Him for the can of black worms only a shocking birth could pry open.

I was on such a high the first few days after Teresa's amazing birth. Recovering from a brutal C-section, I barely noticed the pain. I was too enamored with the five pound, nine ounce bundle of joy in my arms. Teresa was born small but like her Daddy, had very long legs. With little fat on her tiny body, the heroic mother in me rose to the occasion and proudly nursed my first baby!

At first nursing was difficult because my milk ducts were damaged from the implants. My right breast more damaged than my left, Teresa screamed her lungs out when she didn't get enough milk. Frustrated and overwhelmed, I bawled my eyes out while trying to read through books about breastfeeding. Finally, after a couple of weeks, I started to get a system down.

Breastfeeding my baby suddenly became the most beautiful experience of my life. Drizzling quiet mornings to nurse to, I snuggled up with Teresa under a big soft blanket while she sucked to the gentle sound of rain. The safety and comfort I felt was indescribable. Not only was I giving my child the gift of nutrition and warmth, I was using my breasts for something beautiful. No longer were they objects of abuse; my breasts gave life to another human being. I felt so amazingly feminine.

I also felt extremely depressed at times. At first I was mad at myself for not constantly being in joy. But then I read about postpartum depression and figured that was why I was so depressed. When the harsh symptoms didn't go away and nightmares began to appear, I knew something was wrong.

Trauma enters.

Every time I held Teresa I had to fight back tears. The overwhelming realization that my mother never loved me the way I loved my baby began to torment me day and night. Images of my mother's face screaming at me entered my mind.

"You forgetful lazy girl, you never clean your room!"

"Why can't you be more like your sister?"

"Shame on you for talking back to me!"

"Shame on your for not honoring your parents. The Bible says you won't live a long life you know!"

"Don't you know you could go to hell for that?!"

The little girl in me cringed at the tormenting words of shame, guilt and threats my mother barraged me with much of my childhood. The resounding gongs of her nagging voice during my teenage years were even louder.

"I'll make sure your father hears about this one!"

"Don't you dare or I'll…!"

"I love your sister more than I ever loved you!"

"I see Satan behind those eyes. I'm going to cast the devil out of you!"

And she did. She grabbed healing cloths that we bought from a preacher on TV and threw them on me while she attempted to cast the devil out of me.

"In the name of Jesus come out of her!" she yelled into my face while she brooded over me. Sick of her fat loud mouth and years of emotional abuse, I became the devil she professed lived inside of me. The teenager from hell, I gazed my fierce green eyes into hers and with my best contorted demon face I hissed and growled back, "Get off of me, Bitch!"

My mother flipped out and yelled to my father, "Come quickly, Satan's inside of Shelley!"

My Dad came to my bedroom door, told my mother to get off of me and then he clapped. I smiled and gave my mother a dirty look. My Dad wasn't dumb. At least he knew I had talent.

I hated my mother so much. I hated her with a passion. The hair on my arms stood up like her evil disapproving eyebrows when I thought about her cruel words. Filled with uncontainable rage, I wanted to throw something but Teresa was sleeping in the other room. The love of my child stopped me from having a violent outburst.

Then I thought about my Dad. My father and my hero, he betrayed me. I sobbed again. How I longed for the love of my father. I wished more than ever he could hold me and protect me from haunting images of my mother's abusive words. Suddenly I felt huge amounts of anger toward him.

How could he let her treat me so horribly? I argued in my head. *He must have seen and heard her belittle and yell at me,* I angrily thought. Even relatives knew my mother had a big mouth. But my Dad was stubborn and defended the wife of his youth until the end.

Then I realized my Dad was selfish and in love. He preferred his tools and inventing while my mother stood by him and applauded his genius designs. Physically and emotionally abused by his own father, he enjoyed the ongoing approval my mother gave him.

I could have given him that approval, I thought. I was his greatest admirer. A strong willed creative genius, I was exactly like him.

The little girl in me wept for her Daddy. "That mean mouthed lady stole him from me!" I yelled in my head.

I hated her so much that I couldn't hold back anymore and I threw a vase and woke Teresa.

Great, I thought. Now I hated my mother even more.

I picked Teresa up out of the crib and brought my crying baby over to the couch. As soon as I put her to my breast, she stopped crying. Staring into a dark forest of incessant raining, tears of rejection streamed down my face.

"How could she not love me like I love this baby?" The question burned in my heart.

Then I thought about the Pastor and how he taught about forgiveness. It was the one thing I absolutely refused to do. I could pass almost any test but I couldn't forgive my mother or the men who hurt me. Those two would suffer a lifetime for what they did to me.

A Voice interrupted my thoughts. "But if you do not forgive men their sins, your Father will not forgive your sins."

That put a damper on things to say the least. But I refused to listen to God. I couldn't and *wouldn't* forgive. So I internally suffered as I nursed, cursed and rehearsed every offense ever done to me.

As I became obsessed with thoughts of my past, I began to have violent outbursts and verbally abuse Garrett. In fact, I blamed Garrett for everything wrong in my life. It was his fault if I was having a bad day. If it rained, it was his fault. If there was no money, it was his fault. When I had nightmares and flashbacks, it was his fault if he didn't comfort me enough. Depressed for weeks at a time, I blamed it on him for being gone so much. The bitterness inside of me became unmanageable and Garrett was at his wits end.

At the same time I was blaming and hating everyone, my mother began to reach out to me. Of course she did, I had just given birth to her first legitimate grandchild and she was a proud grandmother. So, she threw me a baby shower and I flew down to California with my six-week old baby. I held my tongue, showed my baby off, opened up beautiful gifts from relatives and most of all, I got to see my Italian Grandmother, Teresa. Yeah, I called her Nonnie but her real name was Teresa. I loved her so much I named my baby after her.

I was decent to my mother and even grateful she reached out to me. *Maybe she had changed*, I thought. Unfortunately, it wasn't enough to make up for the onslaught of verbal abuse of the past. She still *owed* me something.

When I got back home things became worse. Seeing my mother again and my family brought back even more memories to haunt me and I fell apart. It didn't help that Garrett's mother still couldn't stand me either. I felt like everyone hated me, including myself. I was ugly, unworthy, and unlovable. I couldn't shake the deep-rooted belief that nobody loved me. I didn't even believe Garrett anymore.

I started working at the Mexican restaurant a couple months after being home with Teresa. The change of environment gave me a chance to breathe but unfortunately I breathed in a little too much of the Tequila air and soon I fell. I started drinking again in between nursing my six-month-old. Wrestling with my two favorite addictions; I juggled breastfeeding and alcohol.

Then I became *more* depressed.

Alcohol only made things worse and I began to spiral out of control until I hit the bottom of 1997. With Teresa's first birthday around the corner and a strong determination to make a New Year's resolution, I ended up in the Army mental health clinic, the Department of Behavioral Health.

It was time to get some professional help, I thought.

"Shelley Lubben." The nurse called my name. The world around me was excruciating. Screaming children and families burned out from military life, I walked through the cold corridor into an empty room and waited for a psychiatrist. A stack of tall brochures on the table, I thumbed through pamphlets about depression, which only made me feel more depressed. I noticed out of the corner of my eye a book about Schizophrenia sticking out of a bookshelf. Gulp.

I definitely didn't want the doctor to know I heard voices.

Out of the blue entered a tall powerful man dressed in an Army uniform and I immediately felt anxious. He introduced himself and pulled out a notebook and pen.

"Tell me what symptoms you are having, Mrs. Lubben."

I was so afraid to tell him, especially about the nightmares and flashbacks. I wanted to run out of there so badly. But I was desperate for help.

"I have nightmares, flashbacks, chills and feel like something is strangling me at night. During the day I am really sleepy and very depressed."

"Do you want to kill yourself?" he asked.

What, is that a trick question? I thought.

"Are you going to put me away for anything I say?" I asked him with lifted eyebrows. I wasn't dumb enough to end up in the crazy ward.

"Well, if you are currently hurting yourself or others, yes, we will have to check you into our inpatient program where you will receive medical attention."

"Well, I am currently not trying to kill myself but yes, I have had thoughts of death in the past."

"Have you tried to kill yourself before?" He stared at me blankly. Okay, now I had to be careful. I shifted to the other side of the chair and casually covered the scars on my wrists.

"No, I haven't tried to kill myself before," I lied. I had to. I wasn't going to lose my baby over stupid questions. I just wanted some medication so I could have some relief.

"Tell me about your past."

Oh wow, I thought. *How much time does this guy have?*

Suddenly the words came out of me, "I was a dancer for eight years."

"Do you have any physical pain from dancing?"

Of course I do, I thought.

I went on and on about my left hip, my left shoulder, my lower back and my neck. I told him I was in pain twenty-four hours a day and that I hurt my left shoulder when I got really drunk and dove into a stage at a topless bar.

"Do you drink alcohol?"

"I've been sober for about two weeks."

"You're probably still experiencing alcohol withdrawals. Did you do other drugs?"

"Um, yeah, I did all kinds of drugs. The main drug I recently did was speed. I quit that three years ago though. I don't feel cravings for drugs. But I definitely crave alcohol. But I'm trying not to drink for the baby."

"That's good, Shelley. Tell me about your nightmares."

I couldn't speak.

"Shelley, can you talk about your nightmares?"

A terrible pain formed in my throat and a huge deafening voice pushed its way out of my mouth and suddenly I blurted out, "I dream about men stuffing their big penises down my throat and choking me!"

Then I vomited out every horrible thing I ever did in porn and prostitution.

While I was trying to get my words out through blubber and spit, I noticed he dropped his pen and laid down his notepad. That couldn't have been a good sign.

At the end of the long session, which felt like it lasted five hours, he diagnosed me with Bipolar Disorder, Impulse Control Disorder, Alcohol Dependence, Depressive Disorder and Post Traumatic Stress Disorder. I was prescribed Zoloft for depression, Antabuse for alcoholism, Naproxen for joint pain, sleeping pills and an eternity of counseling.

Okay, now I'm officially insane, I thought. At least I had the satisfaction of knowing I was insane. I was starting to think I was still demon possessed or something.

An evil voice chuckled within.

The Army psychiatrist wrote out my prescription and sent me over to the anger management counselor and the SAD help desk. I was also diagnosed with Seasonal Adjustment Disorder. Due to three hundred dark days a year in Washington State, ya think?

With appointments made for anger management counseling and "light" therapy, I went down to the pharmacy, grabbed my drugs and headed home in the rain *again*. I really missed California.

Couldn't it just stop raining for one day?" I asked God.

A Voice interrupted my thoughts again, "Shelley, didn't you read my Book?"

I would have thought it was Schizophrenia after reading the pamphlets, but the Voice was too nice to me. I could never be that nice to myself. Anyway, I knew Who it was. God Almighty had been talking to me for years.

"Of course I read your Book, God," I answered Him flip-pantly.

"Read it some more. I have much I want to teach you." Then He was silent. God's still but small Voice was always short and sweet to me.

Next Sunday I was back in church and the Pastor began his sermon as usual with the explosive words, "Success begins on Sunday!"

I wish I could be successful, I thought.

Pastor Kevin instructed the congregation to turn to Joshua 1:8 and after a minute uttered out the words, "Do not let this Book of the Law depart from your mouth; meditate on it day and night, so that you may be careful to do everything written in it. Then you will be prosperous and successful."

"Gee, didn't God just tell me to read His Book?" I mumbled to myself. So I went home and made a new commitment to read the Bible again.

Just as soon as the anti-depressants kick in, I promised myself.

I was weak. I admit it. I was extremely tired too. It wasn't easy trying to raise a baby and a nine-year old while working at a restaurant where alcohol was readily available to numb the traumatic wounds of my past. It wasn't easy one bit. In fact, it was hell and I didn't know how I was ever going to make it.

But the powerful words of the Pastor repeated in my head, "There's a Champion inside of you!"

Maybe he was right, I slightly hoped.

But old negative thinking kicked in and I whined to myself, "But I don't *feel* like a Champion." Then I thought about all the crap I felt like twenty-four hours a day with no help or hope in sight.

Apathetic to my pity party, God interrupted in a thunderous Voice with the words, "For we walk by faith, not by sight!"

2 Corinthians 5:7 resounded in my head as I scribbled it down and smacked it up on my wall.

There, I thought. *Now it's up on my wall where I have to look at it every day.*

Satisfied with myself, I walked away not knowing that Scripture would become the first of hundreds pinned to my future walls. Recovery themed wallpaper, God was determined to turn me into a Champion.

It was only a matter of time.

A good battle plan that you act on today can be better than a perfect one tomorrow.

- General George S. Patton

Sober, sedated and ready to move on with God's plan for my life, I made a call to the military on-post housing to see if our rent-free three-bedroom house was available yet. After a year of waiting and praying to move on to the Army's Fort Lewis, where the grass was greener and the groceries were cheaper, it was finally our turn!

It was a dream come true for a dirt-poor military family.

When the lady on the other end of the phone told me our number was 517 on the list but for some "strange" reason a house became available for us anyway, I knew it was God.

Good old God coming through for me again, I thought. While I proved my potential and passed tests, He proved faithful.

Our new house on Davis Lane was a mansion compared to the small apartment we were living in. Three big bedrooms, utilities paid and a big green backyard with fir trees, I was in green Army paradise! I humbly thanked God and thought about all He had done for me in such a short time. I knew I didn't deserve it.

Over two years out of porn and alcohol free, I loved my new street I lived on. The laughter of children and voices of Moms chatting on their front porches, I finally felt part of a family. Accepted into their world, it was the first time in my life that other women actually liked me. Of course, I neglected to tell them that I was a recovering ex porn star!

Are you kidding?

Anyway, I was a Champion living the Champion life where nothing was impossible and everything was an opportunity. With my ugly past behind me, I boldly stepped onto my new street and breathed in the fresh cool air.

Washington wasn't so bad after all, I thought.

Still working nights at the Mexican restaurant but without the Margarita breath, I spent my days reading God's Word and raising Teresa. Tiffany was in her new school and *finally* had some friends. Her fourth grade class was much better than her third grade class. At least the Army's school didn't screw up and put Tiffany in the wrong grade again. Yes, that actually happened to Tiffany!

Life was getting better and so was I.

Now if only I could cook, I thought.

Trips to the commissary, the Army grocery store, became my new learning environment and sweet Vietnamese ladies became my teachers, especially about rice and meat.

"Yu shult make glound beef. It's leally goot," one petite Asian lady told me with her hands full of wrapped meat.

I didn't know they wrapped meat, I thought.

But I listened to those sweet Asian ladies and learned a thousand ways to cook ground beef. From crowded casserole, spaghetti and meatballs, to Beef Goulash and meatloaf, the Lord *knew* I hated meat and He still made me cook it.

"Humble yourself in the sight of the Lord and He will lift you up," the Lord whispered into my heart. James 4:7 got me every time!

At first I burned my meaty meals and became very discouraged and wanted to give up. But Garrett was thankful and pretended to love every burnt bite. Then he strongly encouraged me to go back to the commissary to learn some more from the little Asian ladies.

So I went back and this time I worked the nerve up to talk to the meat guy.

"Psst!" I looked around to make sure no one was listening.

"Excuse me, sir, um, why do you wrap the meat?" Embarrassed that I didn't know anything about food or cooking, the meat guy had compassion on me and lovingly explained the world of meat to me.

"No wonder they wrap the meat," I said, nodding my head as he held up a bloody dripping piece of meat.

Comfortable in my new grocery hangout, I began to approach complete strangers asking them what their favorite recipes were. People loved it! They couldn't wait to share their recipes from all around the world with me. On a military base, where there were more foreigners than New York City, I learned how to make everything from easy "company" chicken to Asian beef and noodles. Life was getting better and I was on a roll like butter!

Unfortunately, life got "slippery" after we moved on post and I began to feel so good that I gave myself permission to drink again. It's not like I was a professional recovering alcoholic, I had no one to mentor me and anyway, everybody else was doing it.

Unbeknownst to me, the military base was one big happy hammered family. With husbands gone constantly, military wives huddled together at whoever's house had the most beer. Poor, miserable and lonely, beer and board games became a part of our everyday life.

But I was different. I had a Champion inside of me. With church still on my top favorite things to do, every Sunday and Wednesday I would hungrily seek out the truth asking God to heal me from my past. Filled with loneliness from Garrett being gone, I was forced to learn how to rely on God to fill the void. I knew Him as my Father but now I would learn to know Him as my Friend.

"Abraham believed God, and it was credited to him as righteousness," and he was called God's friend".

I began to understand that He wasn't that mean guy up in the sky but a kind, sweet and caring God. What a realization.

Especially when my Friend God took the loving time to show me what *really* happened when I was in the sex industry. Thoughts of me racing my hot red Miata crossed my mind, when suddenly a clearer vision of angels guiding my swerving vehicle formed inside of me. I was taken aback. Then another time God reminded me of how I walked toward a sleazy motel in downtown Los Angeles and a Voice warned me to "STOP" and I waited. Suddenly a crazy man ran out of the motel with a bloody knife and I turned to run and saw the "Jesus Saves" sign on a building.

Gulp.

Or another time when I drove a hundred miles per hour in the left-hand lane on the 110 freeway and there was a *parked* car in my lane. When invisible hands grabbed my steering wheel and jerked my car into the lane next to me, I was shocked. Scared out of my mind, I looked up in the rear view mirror to see two red lights reflecting off of mine.

God visited me so profoundly that I couldn't even stand up during worship. All I could do was weep at God's goodness. I had absolutely no idea God was with me during those eight years so closely. But He assured me the devil would have taken me out right away if it weren't for His mighty protection. I couldn't bear to think of how many times God saved me. It was probably tens of thousands.

God also showed me how He saved me from HIV. I couldn't take it anymore. I asked God to stop showing me the truth about my past and He did, at least until the following Sunday when He continued to rewind the years and show me the hard-core reality of what *really* happened.

Lie after lie revealed to me, I became the Kleenex queen, wiping the spit and tears off of my face for *years*, not months, but *years*. Whenever Garrett came home from the field and went to church with me, He knew right away to hand me the box of Kleenex.

It was amazing that I was able to serve in the nursery. From almost day one I joined the large church, I was lovingly forced to serve in the Children's ministry. The Champion's Church was as big as it was smart and made it mandatory for all parents who used the nursery to serve in Children's ministry once a month. Go figure -- God would use me even though I was a complete wreck.

The kids loved me anyway. Animated like that cute little girl in first grade, I entertained the little buggers with Noah and his ark animals.

"Hello, kids, my name is Noah and this is my boat!" The kids laughed and loved me as my giraffe puppet bit their little chubby arms. Finally, I had an audience that appreciated me!

The Children's ministry was the perfect place for an ex prostitute to heal from childhood wounds without anybody knowing. I absolutely loved it! I felt so safe and pure around children. God knew I still hated men and needed to heal so He lovingly put me in Children's ministry. What a genius. But I knew deep inside that I was made for something more so I tried to promote myself rather than wait on God. Zealous to use my creative writing gift, I volunteered for the Pastor's writing team within the first year of becoming a member. Something tells me they had a good laugh when they read over my lack of qualifications.

But I was unstoppable due to the beautiful discovery of life I was on so I continued to go forward, God directing my paths like He promised me in Proverbs 3:5-6.

Trust in the LORD with all your heart and lean not on your own understanding; in all your ways acknowledge him, and he will make your paths straight.

I obeyed God and did what His Book said and I practiced His principles on purpose. God honored my small steps of obedience and blessed me with even bigger surprises of success. When I screwed up I simply confessed my sins and trusted in the sacrifice of His Son Jesus to cover me. I figured if God loved me enough to save me from something like porn and even have the audacity to clean me up, I was pretty sure He was serious.

With God on a mission to save me and heal me, who was I to stop Him? I didn't understand it all but I really tried to give my all. I read His Word, I prayed, I humbled myself and trusted in Him through the "icky" moments, like the time I had to go to Army rehab.

Yeah, that was a real bummer. Imagine me surrounded by military men in the ISTOP program, the *intensive* short-term outpatient program. I hated it but I couldn't get a grip on the alcohol so I figured a secular program would help me out. Quite the opposite, after blurting out my sexual trauma to a group of weak men, I continually got asked out.

How appalling, I thought.

At least I didn't call them male pigs anymore. That was an upgrade from last year's thinking and anyway, things were getting better in my life. No matter how bad it seemed or how much junk was in my trunk, I knew God had something better for me.

Better marriage, better life, better health, better sobriety, God had an awesome plan for my life and something told me, I better not miss it!

XXII

★ DON'T LET THE D'S STOP YOU ★

★ *Chapter Twenty Two* ★

My high school transcripts were horrible! I barely graduated with an F in computers, a D in nutrition, and a D- in art, probably due to smoking cigarettes in class. Eleventh grade wasn't any better. An F in U.S. History, D- in basic math, a D in typing and a C- in English. I wondered how the heck I even graduated!

I would have *never* thought I would ever be allowed back into an educational institution.

As I watched Garrett go through college in the military, I felt resentful. While he bettered himself I barely got through Army rehab. While he worked full time and attended college paid for by the military, I stayed at home with kids and worked at a Mexican restaurant while trying to recover from alcohol.

What's wrong with this picture? I thought.

But I didn't know any better until one surprising day when Garrett took me to the military education center to pick up his books. Feeling bad about myself, Garrett noticed my long face and asked me what was wrong.

"I feel like a loser while everyone here is smart and going to school."

"You can go to school," he quickly announced.

"No, I can't go," I sadly replied. "I mostly had D's in high school. I didn't even take the SAT test because I knew I would never go to college. My high school transcripts are horrible," I said as my sad eyes wandered to the ground.

"Shelley," he countered, "don't let the D's stop you. Anyone can go to college if they want to. All you have to do is take the college placement test and they will put you in the classes suited for your level."

"But my level is eighth grade math and *maybe* eleventh grade English," I miserably replied.

Garrett insisted, "Shelley, that doesn't matter. They offer high school level courses at city colleges. Why don't you take a placement test and find out what level you're at? You're so smart, Shelley. You can do anything you put your mind to."

That's what my Nonnie used to tell me, I thought.

"You really think it's possible for me to go to college?" I asked with a thin layer of hope.

"Yes, Shelley!" Garrett's words hit my heart and suddenly the heavens opened. At least that's what it felt like. A gigantic light went off inside of me and led me over to the admissions desk where I asked if I could take a placement test.

"Of course, what day do you want to come in?" The receptionist's beautiful words gave me hope. I asked her for the next available date and she marked it down in her computer.

Wow, maybe there's a chance for me, I imagined.

The next couple of days I stressed out really badly over the placement test but God got me through it and finally the day arrived. Praying and believing for a second chance at education, I walked into the military education center and valiantly took the test.

And you know what?

I PASSED THE TEST!

The college counselor informed me that I was at college level for reading and writing and only in math was I at pre-algebra level. I was shocked beyond words.

Pre-algebra? How is that possible? I wondered.

I barely held back tears in front of the lady while she handed me a catalog of college programs to look over. Too overjoyed to read through the list, I simply chose journalism. I loved to write and I had been writing since I was a child. I thought about the book I wrote in fourth grade. I thought about the B+ in journalism I received in high school; that and Speech were the only two classes I ever received good grades in.

A few clicks on her computer and suddenly I was officially signed up for journalism, and then she informed me about government financial assistance programs. I about fell off of my chair when she told me the government would pay for my tuition, books and even daycare. Furthermore, I learned that I could get student loans with *no credit check* to help support my family financially while I attended school full time!

No credit check? I gazed at her in amazement. I thought it was too good to be true. I pinched myself and then asked if she was sure about the information that she just gave me.

"Of course I'm sure, I'm the guidance counselor." She smiled.

Excited beyond terminology, I quickly drove home, shared my elated news with Garrett and made him take me to the military mall to buy me school supplies down to No. 2 pencils.

Then I made him take me to the eye doctor to get a pair of new glasses. Oh yeah, I completely transformed from pitiful recovering alcoholic to professional college student over night!

Nothing would stop me now, I promised myself!

My first day at Pierce College in the fall of 1998 was so bizarre. First of all, there were no kids. Second of all, I *wanted* to learn. Thirdly, nobody knew my past.

Perfect.

I opened up my book in Spanish class and laughed at how easy it looked. I already knew Spanish pretty well so it was just a matter of figuring out the reading part. I especially loved to show off my Spanish skills in front of the other "white" folk.

"Hola mis amigos, me llamo Shelley." I even had the accent down. I lowered my head and smiled as I silently thanked God for the Mexican bars. Funny how a Spanish class made me thank God for a horrible time in my life. God truly was working all things together for my good like the Pastor taught me from Romans 8:28:

And we know that in all things God works for the good of those who love him, who have been called according to his purpose.

The class ended and I was off to English. I couldn't believe how much I had forgotten from junior high, the *last time* I paid attention in school. From predicates to indirect objects, I instantly fell in love with the English language. I began to write powerful research papers, one of them titled, "The Manic Depressive Temperament and the Creative Artist." Unlike the other young students, I wrote out of personal experience. The teacher loved it and I got an A!

The next paper I wrote was even deeper. Due to my powerful revelation of how real God was, I wrote a paper titled, "The Proof of God's Existence." The class was stunned when they saw all of my intensive research, which included my own findings from a telescope I bought to observe the stars and moon every night. What an amazing time that was with God. He spoke to me profoundly during the writing of that paper and told me that someday He would use me to prove to the world Who He really was. I held tightly onto that dream.

My next class was Math 60, the lowest college math class offered. *Ugh,* I thought. I absolutely loathed math down to the numbered squared root! The elderly one of the class, the only thing I could relate to was the decimals. The old hustler in me smiled when I saw the dollar signs.

Eyebrows lifted.

Overall, my first day in college was absolutely unequivocally the best day of my entire wasted life and I was ready for more! That is, until the homework piled up.

The reality of research papers, math assignments and Spanish homework began to hit me while trying to recover from alcohol and take care of Tiffany and Teresa *and* cook dinner every night. I started to hate the eggshells I made my family walk on!

But I persevered and at the end of the first quarter I earned a 3.73 GPA and made the Dean's list. Amazed by myself, I called my Dad and told him I got an A in algebra. He was especially shocked since he was the one who suffered greatly while trying to make me understand math in high school. Maybe it was the fact that he was trying to teach algebra to a teenage alcoholic.

But I digress.

Overjoyed and on top of the world, I continued on in my quest for greatness. With God by my side and true self-love for the *first* time in my life, I was determined that nothing would stop me, not even my pesky family.

The new quarter began and I finally got to take my creative writing class. I quickly slipped into a chair in the back of the room and got out my No. 2 pencil and college lined paper.

Desperate from years of blocked creativity, I couldn't wait to start writing. The teacher instructed us to write every day in a journal the entire quarter and explained that we should write *whatever* came to mind.

That night I let it go and boy did it flow! From a horrible childhood to my horrific past in porn, the words poured out of me like a wild rushing river. With no thought of the teacher, I wrote down every exploited moment or escapade that came to my unrestricted mind. The poetic writer in me was being revived from sudden death as a child and I felt so incredibly alive. Swirling words and crashing creativity, I discovered I was a colorful potent writer!

Now if only my family realized that I was Shakespeare! Between my extremely needy children and a nagging husband who wanted me to go to bed with him every night at 8:30, I thought I would die!

"I'm a creative writer! I can't possibly go to bed at 8:30. Leave me alone!" I scowled and told him to put our little one-year old monster to bed while I went back to writing. The mad scientist in me had been awakened and no one, not even blood relatives could stop me.

It was my time to soar, I thought firmly.

Anyway, Garrett was raised in a good family and attended Christian schools his whole life and didn't understand me or what I was going through. He was a kind man and wonderful supporter but he couldn't give me what I needed most: approval. I needed approval from God first and secondly, I needed approval from myself. Something I had never done in my 30 years of life.

As I approved myself and soared into greatness, it was not without great struggle. I worked tirelessly and pushed myself beyond human levels I didn't know existed. Up all night on cans of Diet Coke, I worked on and perfected assignments until 3:00 a.m. and then woke up again at 6:00 a.m. to feed my daughters. I became a machine. But I overdid it and fell back into depression and started having horrific nightmares again. Attributing it to stress, little did I know that my writing journal was actually a human can opener.

Maybe quitting my anti-depressant wasn't the greatest idea, I thought. So I began to take my medication again, but not even Zoloft could stop the hand of God from extracting the demons locked deep inside of me. Horrible memories and evil attitudes, my journal would prove powerful as one of the greatest releases of human hell ever recorded.

God was faithful in ways that I never would have imagined. Unfamiliar with His mysterious ways, I fought the hand of God and dove straight for the medication and alcohol. But God would have His way and help me beat my demons. On February 14, 1999, my fourth year into recovery and wedding anniversary, I inevitably became pregnant.

I was livid to say the least. I hated Garrett so much that I hated him until nothing was left and then I re-hated him again. I yelled and blamed him for the pregnancy since he didn't keep his end of the "withdrawal" deal. The night of our fourth wedding anniversary, Garrett and I drank too much champagne and evidently this did *not* affect his ability to reproduce.

I hate him, I thought. *Because of him, I am going to lose everything,* I fumed.

I did not want to be pregnant whatsoever. All I wanted was the 4.0 GPA and to succeed for the FIRST time in my life. For the rebirth of my life to be ripped away from me after all of my hard work, I loathed the air Garrett breathed.

Then I got the bad news.

When I woke up one sick morning and puked my brains out and took a pregnancy test and it read positive, I wrote the following cruel words to Garrett in my journal on February 28, 1999:

Dear Garrett,

I wonder if you know what you have truly done to me. I feel devastated, unimportant, raped, violated, guilty, broken and most of all unloved. I feel sick. I feel raped. I have never been so violated in my life. You stole something from me. You stole ME!

I know I am worth more than the way I was treated on February 14. Someday I will be with someone who loves me but until that day I will sadly exist in your arms and hopelessly devoted to someone who doesn't know what love is. You are not my hero anymore.

Full of hatred toward Garrett, I became distant and even more focused on my course work. I shoved my family completely out of the way and at that point, it was *all* about me. If I had to suffer and be pregnant, everyone was going to suffer with me. That was my horrible attitude.

I tried with every ounce of strength to ignore my pregnant condition and earn the 4.0 I lusted after. But unfortunately, I became too sleepy and sick to pay any attention in class. One year after I began the greatest self-discovery adventure of my life, it was completely snatched away from me. I had to drop out of college.

I hit a new level of depression and couldn't and *wouldn't* get out of bed.

Who cares anymore, I thought. I figured God was punishing me for past and current sins so I might as well just lay in bed while He whipped me to death.

Then God had a talk with me one early morning.

"Shelley," a gentle Voice woke me up, "For I know the plans I have for you," declares the LORD, "plans to prosper you and not to harm you, plans to give you hope and a future."

He reminded me of His past faithfulness and that He was working all things out together for my good. He asked me to trust Him and to lay down my life for my family. It was the hardest thing I ever had to do. Only God knew what I truly gave up in that moment.

Months went by, but I still struggled with alcohol. I had to give up my other medications for the baby which shocked my system into even more nightmares and insanity. My body was used to Zoloft and sleeping pills but now I had to go cold turkey for the baby. Overnight I turned into a hallucinogenic lunatic wrestling demons at every turn. Alcohol fought me hard and won for part of the pregnancy. But I fought back hard too. I read every book on pregnancy I could get my hands on. I wanted to *see* the baby. I wanted to *see* the organs being formed so I could have empathy for the baby. I wanted to love the baby more than anything. But I couldn't. I couldn't love anything but myself in that horribly selfish moment. That was when I discovered how utterly ugly I was inside.

I needed a supernatural miracle but none was in sight.

Garrett was frustrated and afraid for the baby but more than that, he was afraid of me and the hell I would wreak on any family member who came within two feet of me. He prayed and tried to keep peace while I fumed in the corner and wrestled with God.

Finally, a small breakthrough. I watched "A Baby Story" on television and became instantly addicted. The creative monster in me was immediately soothed when I saw the unique ways Moms gave birth to their babies. I wanted to be creative too and continue my artistic journey of self-discovery, so, I decided to have a home birth.

If they can do it, I can do it too, I proudly thought.

I called up a midwife and a whole new world opened up for me. Woman-centered care, I learned about natural herbs and how to create a womb-like environment to give beautiful powerful birth to my baby.

God was faithful to replace my loss with something even *more* beautiful and creative.

No eye has seen, no ear has heard, no mind can know what God has in store, the song "Holy Spirit Rain Down" played over in my mind while I peacefully read through Baby books.

I asked God and the baby to forgive me for my extreme selfishness and I re-committed myself to reading God's Word daily. College had become an idol for me and God was faithful to remove the idol and pour into me the thing I needed most, His Word.

Although I still struggled at times with the alcohol demon, I asked God to protect my baby and to have mercy on me and to help me deal with the mental illness. Haunted by my horrific past, I learned how to cast my cares on Jesus and trust fully in God that the memories no longer defined who I was. God's Word defined who I was. I held closely to the comforting words in 1 Peter 2:9:

But you are a chosen people, a royal priesthood, a holy nation, a people belonging to God, that you may declare the praises of him who called you out of darkness into his wonderful light.

I was chosen by God for such a time as this, I stated to myself as I rubbed my big belly while I listened with a stethoscope to my beautiful baby's heartbeat. I was incredibly grateful to God that my baby was healthy and moving. In tears, I asked God to forgive me for the few times I got drunk during the second trimester. I utterly hated myself and would have killed myself if I weren't pregnant. The shame and tremendous guilt I carried from drinking while pregnant should alone have killed me.

But death couldn't hold down what God had ordained to succeed and on November 17, 1999, surrounded by candlelight and family, I went into labor in my warm relaxing bathtub.

Focused in my mind on controlled breathing and the splendid imagery of a flower opening up, I became one in mind, body and soul. After several hours of concentrated labor, with my hand tightly gripped in Garrett's, I took a last deep breath and gave a forceful long push until I felt my baby thrust into the gentle warm water.

Gasping for air after the powerful feeling of release, I watched my beautiful baby slowly float to the top of the water. Graceful and picturesque, it was the most beautiful moment of my entire life. The gentle sound of rippled water, my midwife lifted my newborn daughter up and gently placed her on my wet chest. Still connected to the pulsing cord of life attached to my womb, she stared into my eyes without making a sound.

The midwife instructed me to blow on her face to stimulate her to breathe but I was too caught up in the moment. It was too incredible to grasp so Garrett bent over and gently blew on our baby's face.

A suspended moment in time, Abigail Lorraine Lubben took her first few exquisite breaths of life. Without a single tear or word expressed, the room was silent as our family sat in awe of the heavenly phenomenon we had witnessed. Filled with deep gratitude to God, we pondered the amazing miracle in our hearts and worshipped.

In that incredible moment I acknowledged the true Most High God in a way I hadn't thought possible and I literally understood in the Book of Revelation why people in heaven will cast their crowns at God when they stand before Him:

And when the living creatures give glory and honor and thanks to Him who sits on the throne, to Him who lives forever and ever, the twenty-four elders will fall down before Him who sits on the throne, and will worship Him who lives forever and ever, and will cast their crowns before the throne, saying, "Worthy are You, our Lord and our

God, to receive glory and honor and power; for You created all things, and because of Your will they existed, and were created."

- Revelation 4:9-11(ESV)

At that marvelous moment I cast my crown before God and dared Him to keep doing the impossible in my life.

XXIII

★ *Admit One* ★

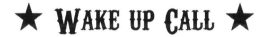

★ WAKE UP CALL ★

★ *Chapter Twenty Three* ★

Big breasted burly whiskered fat fisted Helga the German judge marched into my room and let me have it. She scared the hell out of me.

I should have listened to God but since I had a hard time "hearing" Him on the subject of alcohol, He sent me Helga. At least I guessed her name was Helga. She was a mean German lady on a mission to sober me up.

Drunk and stupefied from a night of heavy drinking, I walked over three miles to the military hospital and turned myself into 5 North, the mental health wing. I was desperate for help because I couldn't stop drinking, even after all the amazing miracles God did in my life. I battled a fierce demon who didn't want to let go of my life. But Helga, a divine messenger from God, gladly scared the alcohol out of me.

She was sent by God. And God meant business.

"How many children do you have?" she asked me in her powerful German voice.

"Um, I have three. I also have a 5 month old. Her name's Abigail," I barely answered.

"Do you breastfeed your baby?" Her eyes squinted and her lips tightened as she leaned forward with her huge hands on her hips.

Intoxicated with alcohol and under the influence of postpartum blues, I cried out, "Yes, I breastfeed my baby. I'm so sorry. I need help for drinking." I bawled my big red eyes out.

Helga looked at me like I was the worst piece of living flesh on the face of the earth and yelled at me for a good five minutes.

"What kind of mother breastfeeds her child while drinking alcohol?" she demanded to know as she pointed her finger at my face. She went on and on about the terrible ways I was damaging my baby's health. Already drunk and severely depressed, she put the final nail in my coffin.

Then she looked over my mental health history and saw that I had been struggling with alcohol off and on for years and she threw down my folder and slapped me in the face with the scariest words I ever heard:

"You will no longer have custody of your children. You are an unfit mother and you do not deserve your babies. I am going to call your husband's commander and he will discipline your husband for allowing child abuse to continue in the home."

I soberly shot straight up and begged her for mercy. I cried and swore up and down that I would do anything it took to keep my children. She ignored me and left the room and I cried out to God for big time mercy.

God didn't answer.

Two men came into my room and told me to sit down in a wheelchair and they wheeled me to an isolated room with no sharp objects in it. Lonelier than any jail cell I had been in, I was in a psychotic hell and at the lowest point in my life.

After I cried myself to sleep and the alcohol wore off, my 6'4 husband walked in the next morning with a face that said it all: he had enough. I knew I was going to lose him and I desperately begged him for mercy and swore up and down that I would do whatever it took to quit drinking.

He didn't believe me.

The timing couldn't have been worse for us. Within two weeks we were scheduled to move to Texas for Garrett's further medical training at Fort Sam Houston. Out of hundreds of qualified soldiers who applied for cardiovascular training, Garrett was one of the soldiers accepted into the elite school. It was a huge honor and high promotion for him and his wife was about to ruin the whole thing for him.

At least now he understood how *I felt* when my schooling was ripped away.

Enraged beyond words, he didn't speak to me at first. I begged and pleaded but he just stayed quiet. The next week we waited to hear from his commander about a phone call from Helga, the German judge and executioner of my life and family. But the phone call never came and suddenly, we were driving away from Washington State to Texas.

Wow, I thought. Was the mercy of God stamped on my forehead or what?

Eternally grateful that God had mercy on me *again*, I vowed to do whatever it took to stay away from alcohol. I stuffed huge amounts of Antabuse down my throat and stayed at home as much as possible. If I absolutely had to go out in public, I refused to walk anywhere near alcohol which was *extremely* difficult on a military base! But I was determined. Even when I went grocery shopping, I never walked through the alcohol aisle. I practically carried a crucifix with me whenever I left the house. I was serious about beating my addiction!

When we arrived in San Antonio, Texas, I was so paranoid to be around alcohol that when a neighbor invited me up for dinner, I asked if they had any booze and when they replied a cheerful, "Yes," I walked right back into my apartment and slammed the door.

I never talked to that neighbor again.

Garrett started his intense 57 week training for cardiovascular technologist and I stayed home and taught myself web design. I knew I had to stay busy if I was going to beat my addiction, so I bought an HTML book and started creating web sites. The creative monster in me was soothed again and the depression began to lift.

I also noticed when I didn't drink that my depression went down about 50%. I should have listened better in Army rehab. It may have been the wrong program for me but one powerful thing they did teach me was that alcohol causes depression.

Now I *knew* they were right!

Far away from the Champion's Centre, it was hard for me to leave but I knew it was God's will. I had made one too many military friends in the lonely wives club and the pity party was over. It was time to focus on my family and completely heal from the wounds of my past. Built up in the Champion Word of God, I would be tested to see if I would apply what I had learned.

God wanted to promote me to the next level but He needed me to pass the test first.

On April 9, 2000, I officially quit drinking *and* cigarettes at the same time. Garrett brought home some of his course work on cardiovascular disease and it scared the crap out of both of us. We threw out his Marlboro Reds and my Capri Lights for good and went straight for hard candy. Lots of prayer and red

Jolly Ranchers, together we stepped out to beat our addictions and better our lives.

Now we were a team. Garrett worked and attended a grueling Army school from 4 a.m. to 7 p.m. every day while I raised babies and taught myself computer languages such as HTML and JavaScript and learned software programs such as Photoshop, Paint Shop Pro, Microsoft Office and more. God lovingly allowed me to do what I loved most: create and learn.

After months of intense training on both of our parts, Garrett was notified we were going back to Washington State where he would later be promoted as a non-commissioned officer in charge of the Cardiology Clinic. God proved faithful once again while we proved our potential. The powerful cycle continued and I began to grow and GROW like a powerful flowering plant, rooted and established in the amazing love of God.

When I arrived back home at the Champion's Centre as a new sober creation in Christ; I was also promoted. The children's ministry needed a new Department head over the four year old class and I immediately accepted. Able to use my creative and leadership gifting, I ran that four year old class like an advanced military operation. Dressed to lead and conquer, I proudly wore my Champion T-shirt as I cheerfully greeted parents and children as they entered my class. In a church of over 5,000 people, I taught hundreds of precious children the powerful Champion Word of God. In charge of everything from writing curriculum, setting up activities and scheduling volunteers, I led over 30 parents every Sunday and Wednesday as we faithfully served in the preschool ministry. With a reputation for recruiting parents and volunteers to serve in my four year old class, I was called the church recruiter. There was no one I couldn't get to serve. If God could use me, I argued, He could use anyone!

I learned a lot about leadership, team work, and how to run a large ministry that first year of leadership at the Champion's Centre. With a hunger to learn and a passion to serve God, I wanted everything He had for me and more! I was unstoppable. I even offered to do free graphic design work and maintain the church web site in exchange for attending Bible school. I was determined to improve myself and continue my education. Little did I know that God had a different degree in mind for me.

With my eye on the prize and God's Word tucked deeply in my heart, I thrived. The Champion life became real for me and God was doing above and beyond all I could ask or imagine just like the Pastor said it would in Ephesians 3:20:

Now to him who is able to do immeasurably more than all we ask or imagine, according to his power that is at work within us, to him be glory in the church and in Christ Jesus throughout all generations, forever and ever!

Amen and thank you for Helga!

★ *Admit One* ★

★ **ACT VI** ★

★ *Meet Shelley #3* ★

XXIV

★ *Admit One* ★

★ BUILDING A CHAMPION MIND ★

★ *Chapter Twenty Four* ★

For God has not given us the spirit of fear;
but of power, and of love, and of a sound mind.
- 2 Timothy 1:7 (NKJV)

In my right and sober mind, it was time to go into heavy battle and conquer the mind monsters that still held me captive. I had passed many tests but now it was time to step up and fight the final battle: getting past my past.

"You can't have a positive life with a negative mind," Pastor Kevin preached during second service. More than anything I wanted to live a positive Champion life but I still had "junk in my trunk" that I needed to face and get rid of.

I thought about my mother. I hadn't forgiven her completely yet. I may have stopped speaking badly about her but I still *thought* bad thoughts about her. The battle still raged in my mind and I had a choice to make: forgive and get promoted to the next level or stay where I'm at and march around the same old mountain.

Tired of being a grumbling Israelite and missing the Promised Land, I decided to put into action what I had learned the past five years and *really* make an effort to not think bad thoughts about those who had hurt me. In fact, I did the OPPOSITE. I began to seek out and look for the best in others on purpose. I thought about my mother and the good things she did for me as a child. I remembered how she took me to the dentist every six months and how I had beautiful teeth because of it. I reflected on the birthday parties she threw for me as a child. I thought about her faithfulness to cook dinner every night for her family and how she cleaned the house. Now that I was a mother of three, I suddenly began to appreciate her more. I understood she made some clear mistakes that hurt me greatly as a child but I chose not to dwell on her mistakes anymore. I realized that unforgiveness was a spiritual and emotional poison and that it hurt me more than it hurt anybody else! Instead of living a toxic life and continue to destroy myself and my family, I began to practice Philippians 4:8 on purpose:

Finally, brothers, whatever is true, whatever is noble, whatever is right, whatever is pure, whatever is lovely, whatever is admirable—if anything is excellent or praiseworthy—think about such things.

I fixed my thoughts on excellent things and when Satan sent mind monsters to remind me of my past, I stood on God's Word and practiced Scriptures such as 2 Corinthians 10:4-5:

For the weapons of our warfare are not carnal but mighty in God for pulling down strongholds, casting down arguments and every high thing that exalts itself against the knowledge of God, bringing every thought into captivity to the obedience of Christ.

I began to powerfully take every thought captive in the name of Jesus. ANYTHING that didn't align itself with God's Word was cast down immediately to the ground. Practicing to think good thoughts on purpose, I didn't realize I was building a strong relentless Champion mind. Twenty-one days to make a habit according to my Pastor, positive thinking started to come natural to me and the blessing of God poured out onto my life.

I started to actually *enjoy* life with my family and began to explore the beautiful wildlife of Washington State where we learned how to fish for salmon, dig for clams, shuck oysters and catch red rock crabs. Light years away from the old world of darkness, God used His exquisite nature to heal the broken little girl in me. Able to run and play in the sand, I lived out a second childhood on the squishy shores of Puget Sound. Shovels and buckets in hand, my venturesome family hurried to dig down deep to catch the rapid Razor clams and long-necks.

Sometimes you have to dig deep, I thought to myself as I held a giant clam in my hand.

God used the wonder of His nature to speak to me profoundly, especially when I tried to shuck oysters. Greedy to finally eat seafood again, I tried with all of my strength to open those obstinate oysters but they were hard to open!

"Shelley, you're just like that oyster." God confronted me on the deeper areas of my life that I wouldn't let Him open up and heal. When Garrett saw me walk off alone over the sandy hills, he knew God was leading me to a healing moment. Standing on the edge of the salty waters of Puget Sound, I allowed God to reach into the darkest places in my heart and expose the ugly lies I believed about myself.

Huge salty tears pouring out like waves, God assured me He threw my sins out as far as the east is from the west. The tremendous shame and guilt I carried for so many years was being literally washed away into the Pacific Ocean. I was no longer a broken child of sexual abuse but a cherished Champion daughter of the Most High God.

My Dad made the heavens, I thought as I sniffed up tears beneath the soft comfort of the white cotton clouds. Amazed by the beauty that surrounded me, I wondered how anyone could deny God's existence.

Then I reached down to pick up a beautiful long-legged starfish that floated up to me. Wide-eyed and childlike, I picked it up to inspect the gentle movement of its friendly legs. Soothed by the gentle glides, I thought about the gentleness of God.

"Take my yoke upon you and learn from me, for I am gentle and humble in heart, and you will find rest for your souls."
- Matthew 11:29

I found rest in God's gentle arms during those peaceful hours on the beach. Proving to me His personal and great love for me, I began to understand what a Father's love truly was. Unlike my earthly father who was too busy, God was available, tender and concerned with every detail in my life. Finally, I received the attention and approval I always needed. Sad that I missed out on a relationship with God in the past, I recounted the wasted years I looked for approval from men in stripping, prostitution and porn.

What a waste of eight years, I miserably thought as I tossed down a cracked shell to the ground.

But God answered and promised me back, "Shelley, I promise you that not one ounce of your pain will be wasted. I have a powerful plan for your life and will use all of your suffering to help others someday." I held onto His promise.

The drives back home from the beach were just as amazing as the days spent there. An abundance of towering plum trees and emerald green bushes of blackberries alongside of the roads, our family loved to stop and jump out of the car and pick the ripe sweet fruit. Home to some of the world's biggest and best blackberries, Washington State became a fruit paradise for me. Every day during the summer I pushed my baby in the stroller and took my daughters to my favorite spots to pick blackberries. At the end of the season, Garrett bought me boxes of jelly jars and lids and I turned my kitchen into a jelly factory. I proudly named my sweet tasty creation, "Shelley's Jelly" and sent it out to loved ones as Christmas gifts.

People loved my jelly!

When winter approached and I said goodbye to the three months of sunshine I was allowed out of the year, I learned not to complain but to find beauty even during the "winter" times of my life. Still in love with candles, I lit them and placed them all over my house to remind me of the flame growing in my heart. No longer did I need candles to shelter me in a world of darkness but now they served to remind me of the constant flame of the Light of God's love.

In the midst of the healing beauty of God's touch on my mind and life, He began to touch my marriage. For the first time since 1995, I started to really love Garrett. I never allowed my-self to become so close to another human being, especially after all of the pain and rejection throughout my life. But after five long years of struggling and healing from my past, my heart suddenly grew big enough to love and *enjoy* Garrett.

Because I first trusted God, I no longer worried if Garrett would leave me. Because my *life's trust* was in the God of crea-tion and not in a human, I was free to love, enjoy and even make mistakes in my relationships. Whether I made the mistake or Garrett did, together we knew it was all covered under the Cross of Jesus Christ. God had *already* forgiven us for past, current and even future sins. Because we accepted by faith the sacrifice of His Son Jesus, we were allowed the freedom to grow in every area of our life, especially our marriage!

Being married to Garrett suddenly became the biggest joy of my life. I was able to freely love him without hideous reminders from my past. A candle-lit room and a sober and healed mind, I learned how make love God's way, not the world's way. With Garrett's beautiful blue eyes gazing deeply into mine, I allowed him to have full reign over my body and heart. At first it was extremely difficult for me to receive physical and emotional love from Garrett, but God gave me the strength and freedom to *practice* receiving love. Garrett and I also prayed before intimate moments and invited God into our bedroom. Yes, we actually invited God, the Creator of sex!

At first I cried and blubbered like a baby but as God healed me through Garrett's tender touches, I began to feel more comfortable and be able to give back selflessly to Garrett. For several years, Garrett and I stayed away from intimate sex and I won out, insisting on the cold unloving sex I was used to. I wouldn't let Garrett tenderly kiss me or look into my eyes those first years of marriage. Sex was more like a ritual for me. But once I completely sobered up and had enough of the Champion teachings inside of me, I was ready to lay down the "facade" of sex we had been having and really allow Garrett to physically express his love for me. I laid down the old Shelley who got us through the first five years and the new Shelley happily submitted to Garrett's gentle hands and together we discovered the beauty of Holy Spirit-filled supernatural sex!

Amen and praise the Lord!

Red-hot beautiful love was in the air and 1st Corinthians 13 proved 100% true as we practiced God's love principles on purpose:

Love is patient, love is kind. It does not envy, it does not boast, it is not proud. It is not rude, it is not self-seeking, it is not easily angered, it keeps no record of wrongs. Love does not delight in evil but rejoices with the truth. It always protects, always trusts, always hopes, always perseveres. Love never fails.

Our love didn't fail because God's Word never failed. Just like the rise and fall of the ocean tides during clam season, the powerful built up Word of God within me released waves of Truth over the shores of my life. Every lie washed up and swept back into a sea of God's forgetfulness, God's Word returned to me the very thing for which it was sent: to fulfill His purpose for my life.

Swept back by the crashing waves of God's faithfulness and goodness, I was finally ready to enter into the Champion life He had prepared me for.

★ *Admit One* ★

★ THE CHAMPION LIFE ★

★ *Chapter Twenty Five* ★

Humble yourselves, therefore, under God's mighty hand,
that he may lift you up in due time.

- 1 Peter 5:6

It was 2002 and time to fly high. Champions for life, Garrett and I and our children set out to make a new life for ourselves outside of the military. Garrett received news that he was being honorably discharged from the military because of his damaged and worn out back. Poor Garrett's back went out so often near the end of his military career that it naturally trained me to pick up everything off the floor. That was a true miracle considering I was a huge slob when he met me.

Now in 2002, I was a Champion Mom who cleaned and made her home pretty, cooked elaborate meals, created colorful and functional web sites, canned her own jelly, raised beautiful children, served as a leader in a Champion church and even had schooling in her back pocket.

Not bad for an ex porn star.

Seven years of a hard recovery out of hell, I walked out of the Champion's Centre a fully recovered and healed Champion woman. God's Word *really* did do what it said it could do. I was living proof of that.

God healed everything in my life from a non-curable disease, bad programming from child sexual abuse, father and mother wounds, bitterness, hatred, rage, rejection, nightmares from the sex industry, sleep disorder, early cervical cancer in 2001, post traumatic stress disorder, alcoholism, mental disorders, and more. God also restored my marriage and relationships with my extended family. Even my mother-in-law loved me now!

Everything seemed perfect. There was just one little problem. There was NO WAY I was going back to California like our extended families hoped. I wasn't going anywhere near that hell hole again so I *influenced* my husband to take a job in Texas.

Garrett was sure he was supposed to take the job in Fresno, California, but I was determined to never go to California *ever* again! I had worked too long and hard on my recovery to step my newly transformed foot onto the immoral state that was home to the porn industry. No way!

That chapter of my life was over. Anyway, I loved the State of Texas, the last true Christian state in America offering excellent education; I wanted to raise my children with the Texas best. So, I hurriedly drove across country from Washington State down to Harlingen, Texas, near the border of Mexico. I figured I spoke Spanish and I loved Spanish people so it was just perfect. What's more, Garrett got offered big money to move down to Harlingen. Although, I didn't understand why no one else wanted the job but of course I thought it was God's Favor. Near South Padre Island, we could fish and swim and live in a big beautiful affordable house on horse property with orange trees while Garrett made the big bucks. I knew *exactly* what I wanted.

A little Voice whispered, "California," in my ear from time to time but I completely ignored it. In fact, I ignored all the signs pointing to California. With both of our extended families living in Southern California and a high paying job tailor-made for Garrett, I still insisted on Texas. Besides, secretly, I wanted to avoid the seven arrest warrants I left behind in California in 1995. I guess I still needed a little "trust" work in God done in my life. Anyway, I had a Washington State driver's license and didn't have to worry about the mess I left in California.

I would simply and entirely forget about my "former" life in California.

When I arrived in Harlingen, Texas, with the Gypsy Kings playing in the background, I was in heaven as I watched the sun melt along rows of wind-blown palm trees. It was a Mexican paradise. Spanish praise flowed from my mouth as I thanked God for the warm weather and sun!

"¡Alabado Sea El Señor!" I shouted from my mini-van.

No sooner had I praised the Lord when the smell of dirty diapers ascended into the air. I rarely stopped for bathroom breaks in order get to Texas in time for school to start. Little Abigail was barely two and her diapers were seeped with pee. Teresa and Tiffany were pulling their hair out along with our cat Jinx. Yes, I actually drove 2,000 miles over rattle-snaked roads with three kids and a cat. It was an insane desperate attempt by a woman who had been released from 300 days a year of dark skies and rain. As the sun greeted me on the palmed covered highway, I sang my Mexican heart out.

I wanted sun more than anything. I loved Washington State but couldn't live one more day in darkness. I needed sunshine!

But as I drove along the highway into town I noticed one peculiar thing. There were no white people, *anywhere*. Now, I felt I was the least prejudiced person in the world due to my past "cultural" experiences but I was hoping that at least *one* person spoke English. I parked and went into the grocery store: no white people. I drove through Chick-fil-A to buy some fast food: no white people. I drove through the broken-down brown mall: no white people.

"Hmmm," I thought to myself.

Luckily, I spoke Spanish and talked with the locals and they all said the same thing: "No hay Hueros aquí." In other words, there are no white people here.

I was going to KILL Garrett. He had visited Harlingen for a job interview and told me it was a wonderful place to live. He even excitedly found a house and put it in escrow to surprise me when I arrived. But when I got there and saw an old house on a dumpy street a few doors away from a junk yard, yep I was going to kill him.

Now I'm stuck in a Mexican hell with three kids and a cat, I thought to myself. It was a darn good thing I knew Spanish.

I angrily called my mother-in-law to vent about her son and she almost talked me into driving all the way back to California. She wanted her grandchildren so bad she could taste them. But God's Word kicked in and I found myself submitting to my husband's wishes. So, I submitted *as best as I could,* right after I yelled into Garrett's ear over the phone. The next morning I woke up in a hotel and got my kids dressed for their first day of school. It was Teresa's FIRST day in Kindergarten.

Distressed by the huge mess we were in, I tried to make the best of it and put on a good Champion attitude. That is until the teacher welcomed Teresa into the classroom.

"Hallo. Belcome to de clase room."

Okay, my kid was there to learn the ABC's, not the "a, be, ce's". There was no way I was going to allow a broken English-speaking teacher to teach my daughter English. It didn't take an ex La Huera Loca to figure that one out. The good mother in me spoke up and asked the teacher if she knew English and she half-smiled back.

"We're out of here," I told Teresa and drove back to my daughter Tiffany's junior high and pulled her out of school.

"What's going on, Mom?" Tiffany asked.

"We're getting the h-e-double chopsticks out of here!" I yelled as I threw the stroller in the trunk. The kids whined and cried while I fumed under my breath. I could *almost* hear God laughing.

Almost.

Then I drove over to the real estate office and told them to put the house back on the market, and that we wouldn't need it. Garrett freaked out because he had already signed a contract with the hospital to hire him as a cardiovascular technician but at that point, the protective mother in me was immovable. We would NOT be raising our children on the border of Mexico after all.

I learned my lesson and made a 2,000 mile U-turn and headed straight to my mother-in-law's house in Chino, California, where most of Garrett's family lived.

But I swore to myself, that Garrett would *still* have to find another job in another state. I wasn't going to *stay* in California.

A few weeks went by and no other jobs opened up. *Dang*, I thought. Suddenly I realized God was involved and that when He gets involved, there's nothing anyone can do about it. You may try to run from God but He will always leave the 99 to come and get you, and if necessary, break your legs.

My Texan legs had been broken while I learned to submit to God's plan in California.

At least nobody knew me in Fresno, I thought.

We hunted around for houses and of course I wanted the big beautiful 3,000 square foot home on the twelve acres of Walnut trees. I wasn't ready to plant my feet in California and buy a house, so we rented a beautiful home in Madera, California. The school was right up the street and the view from my sparkling kitchen window was of beautiful horse property.

It was a mother's paradise.

With two of my precious angelic children enrolled in Christian school and my husband working at the perfect job making TEN TIMES as much as he did in the military, I was a blessed woman. I was so blessed that I was satisfied that I lived a perfect life. Well, almost perfect. I had a heart to preach the Gospel and teach the Champion teachings but wasn't sure where that all fit in. So, instead I spent my time doing web design from home and made pretty good money from it while I *still* put dinner on the table every night. I was a multi-tasking Mama machine!

When my hubby came home after work, I spoiled him absolutely rotten. The man will testify someday I'm sure. He learned very quickly that when Mama is happy, everyone is happy. So, he continued to work hard and make me happy and our love flourished into a wild sizzling love affair. We were so in love, I would have given him ten more babies if it wasn't for the fact I screwed up and made him "fix" himself after Abigail was born. Not to mention, the doctor said after my bout with early cervical cancer I couldn't have any more children.

Anyway, we were happy. We were genuinely happy and I actually didn't have one single problem in the world. Even my parents and siblings came up to where I lived and enjoyed our new life with us. I began to experience the up close goodness and kindness of my mother. She had grown nicer over the years and her charisma lit up the room. Her big personality and beautiful smile, I realized I was a lot like her! My dad, still handsome and more affectionate, had matured over the years and I saw more wisdom on him. I realized I loved them both and truly had forgiven them. It was an awesome time for me.

My parents also spent quality time with their grandchildren. That meant the whole world to me. Finally, after all our family had been through, we were close. One big happy family, I prepared meals and threw most of the parties since I lived right in the middle of California. My brother lived up north and my parents lived down south near my mother in law so my house was perfect! And of course, I didn't mind. I got to show off my cleaning and cooking skills, most of which were inspired by my Dutch mother-in-law. When I first married Garrett, she made it pretty clear I needed to get my act together and learn how to clean and cook. Thanks to her and Garrett taking the time to teach me the Dutch ways, I was never without a rag in my hand.

Okay, I exaggerated a little but seriously I almost always had a rag in my hand.

My mother was shocked when she saw my extreme cleanliness and remarked to my mother-in-law, "Well, at least she listens to you."

Yeah, because she took the time to teach me, I thought. But I held my tongue. In fact, I held my tongue *a lot* during those first few years in California. Of course, I did. I wanted everyone to love the new me!

With a perfect new future in front of me, I never thought about the past one minute. I was on a perfect high in a perfect world and nothing could get me down. Not even the occasional lazy Christian I ran into.

We started attending a Spirit-filled church in Madera that was much different than I was used to. First of all, the Sunday School teachers were always late to class. I couldn't believe it as I looked at my watch every Sunday. The Champion Sunday School teacher in me was appalled.

Secondly, the Pastor didn't teach much of God's Word, which seriously irked me. I thought I would die when he spent most of his time talking about the different demons over Madera.

Like, the devil really cared about Madera that much, I thought.

But the Pastor and his wife and family were really sweet. I figured, anyway, God was probably humbling me for a reason. I suppose I needed it. I was really puffed up in my Champion ways and didn't understand when someone else wasn't excellent. I had been taught excellence in everything I did from seven years at the Champion Centre. I had also attended Wisdom For Life Leadership School where I learned powerful leadership and teamwork skills. The new church I attended now didn't know *anything* about the Champion ways. They didn't even have a worship team for the children! God forbid!

Of course I promptly volunteered to demonstrate to the church the ways of the Champion. But I learned real quickly that some churches are just like average American families, stagnant and unproductive. I wasn't used to living a mediocre life and my Champion methods offended some of the people. Sad and confused by the laziness and lack of excellence towards God's house and people, I was about to quit attending the church when I met a very special woman.

Now she was a Champion.

Her name was Pat and she had a powerful prison ministry. As well as the director and founder of an international Bible school, she held a doctorate in Theology and definitely became my new hero. She was the first woman to come along and really be a spiritual mentor to me on a regular basis. It all started the night she heard my testimony. It was the first time I ever shared my testimony in a church. Of course, I left out the porn part.

"Shelley, you should share your testimony in prison. God has done a lot for you!" she said to me after I spoke. My heart leaped for joy! It was finally the moment I had been waiting for! I had no idea how to share my testimony but I knew I could speak. Then she handed me a prison packet and told me the rules and oh, to bring my California driver's license.

Ouch, I thought. That wasn't going to work. I didn't and couldn't get a California driver's license. My heart sank. I offered to use my Washington driver's license but she said it had to be a California driver's license. My heart sank again.

Out of the blue God spoke to me, "Shelley, go to the DMV and get your driver's license. Trust me."

Um, right, God, I thought. There was no way I would step foot into that place. But after a few weeks of God tugging on my heart to obey Him, I finally agreed to go to the "guillotine" and to trust in Him no matter what. I actually believed I would be arrested and dragged to jail, so I said goodbye to my husband and kids and told them I loved them and that, "whatever will be will be."

The moment I stepped into the DMV I felt extreme personal pain. I definitely did *not* want to or *deserve* to go to jail. I had worked very hard to change my evil ways and now suddenly my entire life was on the line. When I finally got a hold of my arrogant side, I decided to take a martyr's stand and planned that if I got arrested, I would valiantly preach the Gospel behind bars as a prisoner for Christ.

I was next in line. "God, please help me get through this," I desperately begged Him. Then an old familiar voice came along side of me and whispered, "Just lie, Shelley. You can lie your way out of this one." But I rebuked the low familiar voice and chose to tell the truth so help me God.

"Name and social security number, Ma'am?" the placid lady demanded from me. I gave her my information and *then* she asked if I had ever had a California driver's license before.

I paused. The devil leaned forward. God leaned in closer and I gulped and bravely replied, "Yes, I've had a California driver's license before."

Then the lady typed in some numbers, stared intently at her computer screen and suddenly looked up and said, "Please wait here."

Then she walked away. Not good!

As I prepared for the different ways the DMV would cuff me, I prayed again to God and *reminded* Him of His eternal goodness and mercy. Yeah, see, I knew God's Word by now and could repeat His own Word back to Him. God *had* to keep His promises according to what His Word said. I reminded Him of that.

The lady returned and looked up at me and said, "We don't have any record of your previous driver's license so we will just issue you a new one."

Stunned, I put my hand over my mouth to keep from screaming out loud. Who was I to have so much Favor with God??

I tried to remain calm as I received my new paper license while I hid my busting inner smile. I mean, come on, how many people get out of seven warrants for their arrest just like that?

"Ha, ha!" I laughed at the devil as I danced around the DMV parking lot like a Mexican hat dancer. As I did the cha-cha to my mini-van, I praised God in English, Spanish, and whatever Holy prayer language came to mind. God lifted me so high that day I thought I would fly up into the sky!

Surely, God is faithful, I sang over and over as I waved my paper license around in the air while I drove home. People in their cars looked at me like I was nuts. But I didn't care. I knew Who God Almighty was and surely, He was on my side!

When I got my driver's license in the mail, I kissed it and blew a special kiss up to God. "Thank you, Daddy," I whispered. *What a good and faithful Father I have,* I thought.

Driver's license in hand and ready to conquer, I showed up at Central California Women's Facility, in Chowchilla, California, in May, 2003. The maximum security prison was literally facing my back yard. I often thought if the prisoners tried to escape, they'd show up at my house first.

Little did the prisoners know they were in for a huge treat and I, of course, was in for my first real taste of "dirtying" my spiritual hands. Unlike the Champion's Centre where everyone wore stylish Godly clothes and owned shiny Bibles, the inmates were dressed in all blue and carried beat up torn black Bibles.

This place is tough, I thought as I looked around at disasters of women with greasy hair and teeth missing. Even I didn't look that bad after eight years of hardcore hell.

When Pat finished worship and cheerfully introduced me to the prisoners, I took a deep breath, asked God for serious help and bravely walked up onto the grungy stage. With a perfect written outline in my hands, I read every Godly word off of my paper. The prisoners weren't impressed. Some of them even yawned.

Maybe I need to get tougher, I thought as I allowed myself to dip back into the past. So, I put down my paper and blurted out, "I was a porn star who caught Genital Herpes and God healed me."

Gasps from all over the room continued as I shared all that God had done for me. My horrible past intertwined with God's amazing healing of my life, my story turned into a powerful testimony.

At the end of my sermon, I asked if anyone in the audience wanted to know Jesus Christ who saves prostitutes and porn stars and to my amazement, almost all the inmates ran forward and lined up for prayer.

Wow, I thought. *This is the Christian life for me!*

When one rough inmate approached me and wanted prayer for everything from addiction to sexual abuse, I laid my hand on her greasy head and prayed a powerful touch from God over her life. As I prayed against Satan and broke the power of the lies that held her in bondage, I looked down and saw we were standing in a small puddle of tears. I couldn't believe it. The power of God's love had touched the big frightening woman and turned her into a broken bawling child. From that moment on, I knew I was called to the prisons. I began to volunteer every week as a prison counselor where I taught the Champion teachings, prayed for and with inmates, and did inmate counseling.

Now I could pass on to others what God had done for me.

Not long after I started, Pat and her husband moved and left the ministry for me and Garrett to run. When he couldn't join me, often times I was alone and locked down with over 100 prison inmates. But I loved every minute of it! I had never seen so many women so desperate for Jesus in my life.

Elated by prison ministry and encouraged by Pat to continue my education in Biblical studies, I enrolled in the Harvestime International Institute where I learned powerful new teachings. With courses such as Spiritual Strategies for Warfare, Strategies for Spiritual Harvest, Mobilization Methodologies, Evangelism and more, God began to prepare me for a powerful ministry. I didn't know it at the time, but He was on a mission to turn me into an American Missionary.

At the same time I began my Biblical training in Madera, something else happened. The Holy Spirit-filled church I attended announced a special guest speaker would be at the women's monthly meeting. She was billed as a prophetess.

Okay, I thought. *That's weird.*

Aren't prophetesses only in the Old Testament? I asked one lady. She just smiled at me and encouraged me to come and hear the Word of the Lord. So, with my guard up, I arrived on time and sat there with my arms folded. I became especially alarmed when I saw the girl who went up to speak was no older than 25. As if God couldn't use a young woman to speak to me.

But I was set in my Champion ways. I wanted to hear Scripture and wisdom, not some young girl spout her mouth off about what she thought she "heard" God speak.

Suddenly, she began to pace the stage and shouted out to the crowd that the Holy Spirit wanted to move prophetically tonight.

What's prophetic? I thought. Then she began to point to some of the women in the audience and said they were standing out to her like sore thumbs and that God had a message for a few of the ladies tonight.

Unexpectedly, she pointed to me and said for me to stand up, that God had a Word for me. I looked around. She couldn't have possibly meant me.

"Who, me?" I asked. The other ladies made me stand up to hear the Word she had for me.

She began to speak. "The Lord says to you, He has made you bold. In fact, He is making you so bold that I see a picture of you clinking your glass in a restaurant boldly offering deliverance to everyone around you."

I cringed. I vowed to never go out to dinner again. Okay, how could this lady know I'm bold? I had to admit she was right about that one.

She continued, "God says to you that you have a prophetic message for the Church and that church leaders need to listen to you." The leader in me liked that part.

Then she called me up on stage and in front of everyone she told me I had been given a Deborah's anointing and that I was called to be the Church fire alarm and had a powerful message of warning.

Who's Deborah? I nervously thought. *How am I a Church fire alarm?* I wondered.

That's when I started to feel *very* uncomfortable. But the young prophetess didn't seem to care. She made me open my palms and she smacked them down with hers and suddenly an amazing power flowed through my whole body. Then she laid hands on me and "activated" the new boldness in me that God wanted me to operate in.

Then I walked back down the stage in a strange blur and found my way back to my seat. Women around me started poking me saying they were excited about the Word I received while I just sat there.

What just happened to me? I wondered. I felt different and something inside of me was *very* excited. My spirit was leaping inside of me actually. Then the prophetess suddenly called on my daughter Tiffany and told her she saw drumbeats all around her and that Tiffany had a powerful musical gift. I suddenly remembered back to the old days when I walked downstairs to my four year old pounding on my shoe boxes with wooden spoons while she watched MTV.

Tiffany and I just stared at each other. We knew God was speaking to us through that hotshot 25 year old prophetess. I was humbled to say the least.

Now that my theology had been smashed and the meeting ended, women excitedly chatted about their "words" while I quietly grabbed my things to leave.

Deborah, who's Deborah? I thought as I tried to remember her from the Bible. But as I stood there thinking, *another* lady approached me. She was a sweet little old lady that I saw every Sunday so of course, I wanted to be polite and listen to her.

"Excuse me, honey, Holy Spirit says to tell you that you are His Warrior Bride." She smiled and hugged me and then walked away.

Um, okay that was even weirder, I thought as I grabbed my daughter Tiffany to get out of there. The church proved too weird for me and I scrammed home to go and tell Garrett we needed a new church.

When I got home he was asleep and I didn't want to wake him because he had to get up early for work. So, I got on the computer and checked email instead. Tiffany went to bed while I sat up and "thought" about what had happened. I couldn't shake the feeling that every word that young prophetess had said was true.

"Okay God," I finally spoke out loud, "if any of what happened tonight is true, I'm going to need some proof. Prove to me right now it's true and I'll believe it. But I have to know it's you."

God surprised me when He asked me, "How do you want me to prove it?"

I looked up at my computer and saw Google on the screen and so I dared God to show me ONE web page with the two search terms, "Deborah's Anointing" and "Warrior Bride" and that if BOTH of those search terms turned up on ONE web page, I would believe Him. I made it clear to Him that the results had to be on ONE web page, not one web site.

God replied, "Done." So, I pecked away at the keyboard with a half smirk on my face and typed in the two terms in Google and pushed "Enter".

Then I clicked the first link and suddenly my eyes popped out when I saw a web page that read, "Anointed for War," with an article beneath titled, "Warrior Bride: The Four Anointings", and beneath *that* it listed the Deborah's Anointing as one of the four spiritual warfare anointings.

I immediately fell off my chair and worshipped God. That was literally impossible for one web page to show up with all of those terms. When I finally got back up in my chair to read over the web page again, I went back to the Google results and saw there was NO OTHER WEB SITE that listed any of those terms in one single place. Only the one web page had them.

Still shaking my head in disbelief, I searched on Google to learn about the Biblical Deborah. When I read that she led ten thousand men into war, I knew that was me. I knew somehow that's what I was called to do. But I didn't know how. I also read that Deborah was the only female judge, military leader and prophetess and only Samuel and Moses also held those three offices.

Oh, wow, I thought. I was even more humbled. *Who am I to be a prophetess for God?* I wondered in complete awe.

The next morning I got up early to give Garrett an earful of what God did and He just smiled. He already knew his bold wife had a big purpose.

Although I wasn't quite sure what that purpose was, I continued my schooling and volunteered at the prison and local rescue mission until one day Garrett announced we had to move because God blessed him with an even better job. Heartbroken to leave the prisoners and rescue mission behind, I wondered what God was up to. When I asked Garrett where we had to move he replied, "Bakersfield."

Gulp. Why was God moving me closer to Los Angeles?

XXVI

★ *Admit One* ★

★ JOURNEY TO PARADISE ★

★ *Chapter Twenty Six* ★

It was strange to move to Bakersfield. Everything was being handed down to me on a silver platter. First, we bought a house in Bakersfield only a year after I finally broke down and agreed to buy a house in Madera. I figured I loved prison ministry and Garrett had a great job so we might as well settle down there. So, when Garrett came home a year later to tell me he was offered a sales job for a major medical company with an opening in Bakersfield, I was confused.

"But we just bought a house in Madera," I argued.

But he said he knew it was God. So, when we put the house up for sale without a realtor and I did all the legal paperwork myself and then sold it for $100,000 more than we bought it for, I KNEW it was God. What person wakes up one day and decides to sell their house a year later after they bought it and make $100,000 on the deal?

Only God could do that. I guess He wanted us to move to Bakersfield.

The second reason I knew God was up to something was because my spiritual mentor's best friend was the women's director at Bakersfield Rescue Mission and wanted me to be a counselor on the women's recovery program.

How perfect is that? I thought as I dreamed of rescuing women. Yep, God was definitely up to something.

Third, God led us to the perfect house. A four-bedroom home with a big back yard and huge pool, I promised God if He gave me the house I would invite all the rescue mission ladies over for Baptisms and barbecues. He loved my idea.

So, we slapped a nice large down payment, moved in June of 2004 and enrolled our girls into the local Christian school right around the corner. Life could just not be any more perfect!

With money to burn, Garrett and I bought hundreds of beautiful lush plants and assorted rose bushes to design our new backyard paradise. Garrett, a former landscaper and a Dutch gardener, knew everything about gardening. He had spent years dreaming about his ideal garden and now was his chance to design it. It was one of the most special and spiritual times in our marriage. We ended up buying over 20 varieties of roses and I bought a book on how to take care of them. You can imagine the lessons God taught me through pruning.

Garrett also loved palm trees. He taught me how to build a beautiful landscaped pool area with Queen Palms, Birds of Paradise and yellow and red Daylilies. Our backyard looked more like a lover's paradise. The wild Italian in me pitched in and added a little spice to the "perfect" rows of Dutch plants. I wanted trailing Ivy. Garrett wanted colorful rows of Impatiens. We compromised and did both. Together we learned how to build a beautiful wild lush paradise beneath one of the hottest sun spots in California: good old Bakersfield.

It baked us all right. With high temperatures up to 110 degrees during the summer, we swam in our pool every day. And with our extended family close by, we invited them over for barbecues and had the best family times together. My life was absolutely perfect.

Almost every morning we sat outside in our beautiful lush paradise and prayed and thanked God for all He had given us. With the fragrant aromas of Star Jasmine and roses surrounding us, we enjoyed our little piece of heaven on earth.

It amazed me to think about how far God had brought us in eight years.

Now, if only we could find a good church, I thought.

We started visiting churches each Sunday but we didn't seem to fit in anywhere. Either one church was dead in worship or another one was dead in the Word. We wondered if we were being overly critical.

Being a Bible student didn't help either. I heard things in the pulpit that caused me to bite my tongue repeatedly. To ease the pain of church, I started bringing my homework with me and quietly worked on it behind my opened Bible. We started to wonder if we were being hypocrites for playing the role of "church goers" but not getting anything out of the service. We seriously questioned if something was wrong with us.

Little did we realize that God was teaching us some important lessons.

Bakersfield was tough for us. We attended over 20 churches when we first arrived here and although many of them had good things about them, we never found a church that was similar to what we knew and loved, the Champions Centre. We were used to wisdom from the Word, celebratory powerful worship and working together as a team to build Champions in one another. The farmer mentality in Bakersfield simply did not offer that.

"Now what do we do?" I asked Garrett.

"Pray," he said as he shoveled dirt into his last hole.

I began to really cry out to God about finding a church home. We continued our search but found nothing we felt we could call "home". But God kept blessing us and teaching us on our own. We knew He had a purpose in all things so we trusted Him.

But it wasn't easy. I was extremely concerned I wasn't being fed God's Word enough. Then all of a sudden, God blessed me with a special surprise: I got accepted into Vision International University to pursue a Bachelor's Degree in Theological Studies.

A whole new world opened up for me and I began to study hours every day about the thing I loved most: God's Word.

Unbeknownst to me my Theology would get smashed *again*.

One of my first courses on Hermeneutics, the study of the principles of interpretation concerning the books of the Bible, really messed me up. I was flabbergasted and about to sue the entire Christian world when I learned all the different ways to study the Bible through cultural, grammatical and historical methods.

Why have I never heard of these methods before? I wondered in disgust.

I about fell off my chair as I re-studied Scriptures I had been taught throughout my life. I especially fell off my chair when I learned about Hebrew idioms. Idioms are simply phrases. For example, an American idiom would be when we say something like, "it's raining cats and dogs," and we understand that the phrase means "it's raining heavy", but to a foreigner who hears that phrase, he may think it's literally raining animals on top of us. He may not understand it's an American idiom and may need someone to *properly* translate the phrase for him.

Hmmm...

So, when Jesus, who is fond of using Hebrew idioms, says things like, "If your eye is good, your whole body will be full of light," in Matthew 6:22, it's actually a Hebrew saying that means, "if you are generous." It has nothing to do if your eye can see well. Jesus was talking about being stingy versus being generous.

Idioms for Idiots, I thought as I wrote down the title for a future book for Christians.

No wonder the Scripture in James 3:1 reads:

"Let not many of you become teachers, my brethren, knowing that as such we will incur a stricter judgment."

I wondered how many current pastors, bishops, priests and teachers were going to be severely judged for all the hogwash they had been preaching and teaching. I wanted to yell it from the rooftop but God told me to cool it and just learn.

So, I held my tongue, at least for a while.

Eyebrows lifted.

As I studied the Word day and night between laundry loads and taking care of my family, I grew in knowledge and wisdom in ways I would have never thought possible. Something was happening to me.

God began to powerfully visit me.

I suddenly had the urge to study the lives of great reformers such as John Wycliffe, George Fox, John Calvin, John Knox and in particular, Martin Luther, the Battle-Axe of Reform. I laughed when I remembered how Garrett used to call me that name when we were first married.

"You battle-axe!" he yelled at me when I wouldn't shut up. If only he had known.

As I studied the life of Martin Luther, I felt kindred to him.

I even had a last name similar to him, I thought.

(Luther sounds like Lubben) *Maybe,* I thought.

When I read that Luther spearheaded the great Reformation and it literally still impacts the Christian world today, I felt a "strange" similar call on my life but had no idea what it could be. Then I read that Luther often stood alone, lost friends and family, stirred international conflict, angered leaders of nations, and created chaos for the Roman Catholic Church.

Gulp. I didn't want to lose everything I loved and held dear. But I couldn't deny the major attraction I felt toward the words, "The Great Reformation."

As I continued to hungrily study the lives of powerful ministers and great reformers, I also latched onto who would become my favorite all time mentor and preacher, Charles Spurgeon, also known as "Prince of the Preachers."

Now, I could go to his church! I thought.

It was a shame he was dead. It seemed like all the great preachers of the Gospel were dead.

Great, all of my mentors are dead, I thought.

I hung out at Spurgeon.org for years and bought Charles Spurgeon books and soaked myself in hundreds of his sermons. He preached over 600 sermons before the age of 21! I couldn't get enough of him!

Yes, I became a Spurgeonite.

I also studied the phenomenal lives of Martin Luther King Jr., Billy Graham and one of my personal Catholic favorites, Mother Teresa. She is one of my greatest mentors who taught me about love, patience and humility.

Finally, I was being fed MEAT, and not the milk that most churches offered. I started to understand that God was calling me into a deeper and higher time of learning in the knowledge of Him and that it *may* be the reason why a church home didn't open up for us.

That's when God *really* visited me.

I began to spend hours alone with God listening to His powerful Voice speak to me through the natural paradise in my backyard. As I admired our beautiful new grapevine trellis, I thought of the powerful words of Jesus in John 15:

"I am the vine; you are the branches. If a man remains in me and I in him, he will bear much fruit; apart from me you can do nothing."

I held the green soft vine in my hand as I thought about the Lord's serious words to me. I never wanted to do anything apart from Him. I had already been to hell and back and wasn't interested in ever leaving the Lord's side.

The Lord also talked to me through the fruit trees we planted. The first year there was no fruit but as we obeyed and followed Him, we began to see small fruit pop up on our lemon, lime and apricot trees. It was amazing! Our backyard turned into a prophetic symbol of the work and growth that God was continuing in our lives.

When the dead leaves needed to be cut off, God would speak to me about dead areas in my life. I was never without cutting shears when I was in the garden. We had planted so much that God could literally ask me to cut off dead things every day!

Then of course, there were the weeds, the things in life that choked me that needed to be removed. God opened my eyes to show me these areas which were very difficult to understand at the time. But I obeyed the Lord. I started to remove unholy things in my life, even unholy relationships. That was very hard for someone who wanted to be "loved" so much. But I wanted God's Presence more than anything else. I remembered my Grandfather's last words he said to me, "Practice the Presence of God, Shelley."

Between 2002 and 2004 it was a powerful time of consecration for me. I practically became a monk. I didn't listen to secular music. Actually, I hadn't listened to it in eight years. I never watched television. I didn't speak one vulgar word or practice any worldly ways. I could even go a whole day without sinning. Of course, anyone could do that if they spent all day with God for several years in a paradise.

I was spoiled absolutely rotten with God's Presence. Between the nature in Washington State and the paradise in my back yard, I grew to treasure God's Voice and it was the MOST beautiful thing I had ever heard or experienced. I loved God's Voice so much that I diligently spent three years studying His Voice through my schoolwork, prophetic workshops and on the Internet. I wanted to read *everything* and learn *everything* I could about God's Voice.

I fell madly in love with the God of Creation and all I ever wanted was to be with Him. I called Him, "Abba", the affectionate Hebrew term that Jesus also used meaning, "Daddy".

Abba was my Daddy.

Gradually, I stopped wanting to be around people very much. I wasn't interested in the normal things other people were interested in. I didn't want to attend tea parties at women's Bible studies. I didn't want to listen to some preacher talk about the Super Bowl from the pulpit. I especially couldn't tolerate it when I heard Christians share their eternal joy over their favorite TV shows. How easily their faces lit up over those things rather than the things of God.

Ugh!

I just couldn't tolerate the outside world in any shape, form or fashion so I stayed inside or in my garden all day listening to God share His secrets with me. It even became a little difficult at times to have a healthy marital relationship with Garrett. There I was in the Presence of God Almighty listening to the profound mysteries of Christ and Garrett wanted romance. I suddenly understood why Paul said about single people that it was "a good thing for them to remain as they are, as I do."

But Garrett understood. Even he couldn't deny that God Almighty was TALKING to me on a regular basis like He did with Moses or Abraham. Awakened often in the night with God's Spirit hovering over our bedside, Garrett knew I had tapped into the "other" side in a literal and profound way. Plainly, I had become God's friend and God wanted to talk to me. All He ever truly wanted from the beginning was a friend, He told me. I vowed to Him I would always be His friend no matter what.

"No matter what, Shelley?" He asked me.

"No matter what!" the zealous Peter in me promised.

Then out of the green garden fall in late 2004, God whispered into my ear, "Tell your story." I knew what He meant. God wanted me to put up a web site and tell my *whole* story.

"Uh, no I can't do that," my heart quickly responded. I had already shared my story enough with hundreds of women in the prisons and rescue missions. Besides, I already had a ministry. Preaching and teaching the Word once a week to women in recovery, I was happy where I was at. Anyway, I wasn't going to ruin my perfect holy life and go public about my "porn" past.

Are you kidding?

I can't do that, I told God and then I argued a million good reasons why not.

First of all, I didn't want to deal with ugly mean people. I *knew* the porn industry would attempt to crucify me if I ever came out publicly with my story. I imagined all the vulgar words and things they would do if I exposed their evil deeds. Besides, I definitely did *not* want to die with the ex porn star label imprinted on my gravestone. No way.

Secondly, I was the cupcake queen and field trip Mom at my children's Christian school. The teachers all knew and loved me and I had made wonderful friends with the other prestigious mothers.

Thirdly, I enrolled my teenager into a private elite Christian high school and did not want the kids to mess with her *at all*. It was also her first time to have a chance to use her drum skills and she became a percussionist in the elite school's band.

Fourthly, my husband worked with doctors and professionals who we definitely did not want to know my past.

Fifthly, I may lose the family relationships I worked so hard to build.

And that was only the beginning of the dozens of excuses I gave God as to why I could not and *would not* put my "story" up on the web.

I took a last stroll into my evening garden paradise for a final breath of the fragrant fall air and then I went in for the night. It was time to snuggle up with Garrett in my big comfy warm bed and study my Complete Jewish Bible along with my Wycliffe Bible Commentary.

I couldn't wait to see what God would show me tonight!

XXVII

★ *Admit One* ★

★ TO HELL WITH PARADISE ★

★ *Chapter Twenty Seven* ★

The Spirit of God abruptly woke me at 3:30 a.m.

"Put up a web site with your story."

I finally agreed. "Okay, God."

One thing about me, I don't argue with God at 3:30 in the morning, especially when His Spirit prompts me, comes upon me and empowers me to put up a web site in three hours.

I was a web designer. I also knew how to do search engine optimization and so of course, I conveniently neglected to do that part. I figured, nobody would find the web site and *if* they did, maybe it would help some women leave the sex industry. So, I purposely left the Meta tags blank.

Smile.

Of course, none of that in the slightest way affected God. He could do whatever He wanted and He did. Within a couple of months, "stragglers" began to find me. I know because I used a stat counter to keep an eye on how many people visited my new web site.

I was naughty, I admit it. I really was *not* ready to share my story with the entire world.

I got away with it at first. But soon I started receiving emails with requests to do online interviews.

"Okay, God, I guess it's time to talk to my kids and schools about Your plan," I told God.

"Yes," He lovingly replied.

So, after having a discussion with my family about God's intentions, I ended up at the principal's office of my children's Christian school. To get it over with, I blurted out what God told me to do and that I was a former porn actress and that God saved me from everything under the sun. To my great surprise, the principal smiled and told me that he was an ex heroin user and his mother had been a prostitute!

Thank you, Jesus, I thought.

Soon the entire school knew about my story. Moms and teachers began to come up and say they were touched. The librarian was especially heartfelt and cried tears over what God had done with my life.

I began to truly understand that my story was touching many different lives. I already knew my story helped women who were wrecked from drugs and alcohol, but to positively affect the lives of good Christian women, this was a surprise to me.

God continued to astonish me until one day the organization, "Morality in Media", asked me to do my first online interview. I thought I had hit it big time. Finally, I would share my story with the world and everyone would come to know and love my Jesus! So, I did the interview *very naively* and honestly had no idea what I was getting into.

During that interview I was asked about my feelings on porn addiction. "Porn addiction?" I asked her. "What's that?" I had no idea what she was talking about. I had been locked inside of a Christian bubble since 1995 when I started attending the Champion Centre. I had no idea what porn addiction was.

Although I did web design, I never hung out at social networking places. I only hung out at web design forums with other web designers. No one ever talked about a porn addiction. We talked about coding.

So, I was completely hidden from pornography and most of the world for over 10 years. The closest I ever got to the contemporary world was when I went to the grocery store *after* we left the military in 2002 or when I worked with a customer on their e-commerce web site. I didn't watch TV, except children's shows like Barney. I didn't listen to secular music or the radio. I raised my kids, studied God's Word and Theology, taught Bible classes at the rescue mission and designed web sites.

I lived a quiet and comfortable Christian life and suddenly the lady on the other end of the phone was interrupting it.

She explained to me that pornography addiction was the number one mental health problem and proceeded to share horrific pornography statistics with me. I sat back in my chair and gasped. I was stunned to hear that millions of pages of porn were up on the Internet. I was horrified to learn that the porn industry released 11,000 movies versus Hollywood's 400 per year. I was even more traumatized to learn that 54% of the pastors had viewed Internet pornography within the last year.[29]

"Pastors?" I asked, appalled. I truly had been reformed into a nice Christian lady who had completely forgotten her past. I assumed anyone who was a Christian leader lived a good and holy life. How a man of God could *ever* view porn, was beyond my limited holy thinking. God would surely zap me if I *ever* did a thing like that!

After the interview I was upset. In fact, I was downright angry. How could the Church and the government allow the porn industry to get away with so much murder? Didn't they *know* the truth about pornography and that the women in porn didn't enjoy making porn?

I sat there and fumed and God spoke clearly to me and said, "Shelley, you should write an article about the truth behind the fantasy of porn."

Suddenly, Holy indignation filled me and I was scribbling down a mildly graphic article about the truth behind the fantasy of porn.

The article frightened me. I had never written an article in my life except research papers. It definitely was my first "graphic" article. *Woe, unto me,* I thought. *I have lost my mind.* But God assured me that HE wrote the article through me.

Then He did something crazy that I shall never forget. Suddenly, the lyrics, *"You make a grown many cry"* played in my mind and it frightened me so much that I shoved the explicit article away from me. Why was a secular song playing in my mind? Surely I hadn't heard the song, "Start Me Up" in many years. But God assured me He had His reasons for using a Rolling Stones song to speak to me. Then a Scripture came to mind when Jesus spoke in Luke 19:40:

"I tell you," he replied, "if they keep quiet, the stones will cry out."

Wow, I pondered in my heart. God Almighty just used a rock-n-roll song to speak to me. Surely, my Theology was completely crushed by now.

But I obeyed God, put the article up online and almost overnight my "Truth" article began to circulate throughout the world. My web visitors went from hundreds to thousands by the end of 2005. Suddenly, churches, organizations and porn-affected people all over the world began to contact me. The porn industry *also* contacted me.

Now, *they* wanted an interview. I actually was excited because I truly believed I would get them all saved in one interview. I was so excited to show them the love of Jesus and offer them hope and healing.

Luke Ford, nice guy and porn journalist, began the interview by asking me what my stage name was.

I shyly answered back, "Well, I've never revealed that."

I actually hadn't put up my "porn" name on my web site because I didn't want people who visited my web site to be tempted to look at old movies. But I figured that since Luke's web site was an "adult" blog that nobody from the Christian world would ever read it. Plus, I had received emails from pornographers by now that told me I was a liar. So, I figured it was the perfect time and place to divulge my former work name and "shut the mouths" of the naysayers.

"I went by the name Roxy," I confessed. Then I shared the PG version of my experience in porn, not wanting to "offend" anyone in the porn industry. I was *very* new to the modern world of porn in 2005.

I thanked Luke for the interview and excitedly waited to hear the warm responses from the porn industry. Here's a small sampling of what I received:

"You stupid bitch. Nobody cares what a washed up whore has to say."

"F—king liar. You're still an attention whore."

"You're nothing but a Jesus f—king whore!"

I freaked out. I couldn't believe the evil comments that jumped out and attacked me through my computer screen. Then the vicious emails came. Pornographers and pro-porn promoters began to threaten me flavored by every evil vulgarity from the pit of hell. I became totally overwhelmed.

I wept on and off the entire year during my crude awakening in 2005. I didn't understand how people in the porn industry couldn't see the beauty of what God had done in my life. To make things worse, so-called Christians and "religious" people sent brutal emails of rebuke and an endless chain of suggestions about what I should or shouldn't do in my new "porn" ministry.

To add injury to insult, I sent my parents and family my testimony right after I put up my web site in hopes they would glorify God with me and even celebrate how He was using me. I was rudely awakened when my mother told me I was probably listening to the voice of the devil.

"WHAT?" I couldn't believe it. My own mother turned on me after all the recovery I had done. Then, she began to share with other family members the horrible "attack" I had launched on her and my father. Furthermore, she got my brother and sister involved and certainly, I was privileged to read their emails of rebuke along with all the others I received.

Of course, I wrote back and defended myself and suddenly I was in email hell. There went all that wisdom I gained from the Champion's Centre.

In the same year that Satan launched a brutal attack on our family, my husband's dad died on April 1, 2005, in a freak bike accident. Everything around us completely fell apart and our perfect paradise was entirely ripped away from us.

We were literally living out the Book of Job in the Bible.

Undone and completely broken, I cried out to God for answers. Out of the blue on the internet, a kind woman instant messaged me and said God told her to give me Isaiah 26:3:

You will keep in perfect peace him whose mind is steadfast, because he trusts in you.

I was *greatly* comforted. I held fast to that Scripture and applied it to every foul and ugly thing that came my way.

That's when the devil paid me a visit.

The night was dark and cold. All of my children and husband were tucked in bed while I was, of course, reading through emails. A terrible heaviness came over me and suddenly I felt my body trying to faint.

Faint, I thought. *I never fainted before. What's wrong with me?*

When I got up out of my chair, I realized some THING was on top of me and was squeezing my head. I realized what "it" was and rebuked it in the name of Jesus while I tried to walk to my bedroom to get my husband to pray for me. Thrashed around by an evil entity from wall to wall, the wicked force wrestled me to the floor where I passed out near my five year old daughter's bedroom.

We don't know how it happened, but *someone* dragged me into my room and placed me under my ironing board. Suddenly, I heard Garrett's voice calling my name and I woke up and turned my head to see a pair of eyes looking back at me. My picture of Jesus had somehow fallen from the wall and now it was staring straight at me. In shock from everything, I tried to get up but the heaviness was still on top of me and I felt like I was being strangled. Garrett, an ex combat medic, thought I had some type of physical ailment but when I barely squeezed out the words "Satan" while pointing to my throat, he started to figure out that *maybe* it might have been demonic. I gave him a crazy look like, WHAT ELSE COULD IT BE, IDIOT??

Garrett rebuked the evil thing off of me and finally, I was able to breathe. I was so terribly frightened that I grabbed every different version of the Bible I could find and hurriedly hid under my covers where I repented for every sin I had ever done since three years old.

I was TERRIFIED!

I fearfully cried out to God, "Abba, God, please save me!" But God assured me there was nothing to be afraid of and that He was right there with me. He reminded me that Satan had no authority over our family and to use the name of His Son Jesus and rebuke him. Suddenly I remembered spiritual warfare Scriptures and began to recite them out loud where EVERYONE including the devil, could hear me. Scripture after scripture I declared in the name of Jesus until I finally became tired and fell asleep.

That is, until Satan woke me up. My eyes shot open when I somehow felt a huge ball of floating black enter my room and hover over the edge of my bedside. Then I heard a voice speak the literal and forceful words, "This is my world system and you're not going to f—k with my system."

Those were the devil's exact words. I immediately looked up at God and felt His great Presence enter me. Full of the Holy Spirit I turned my head toward the devil and boldly replied, "Talk to Jehovah," and poof, he was gone.

That first year of battling Satan would be the first of many years of warfare ahead for our family. Untrained in the strategies of the adversary of the Saints, little did we know that the battle against Satan's Kingdom and for millions of precious souls, had only just begun.

XXVIII

★ TIFFANY'S PAIN FROM PORN ★

★ *Chapter Twenty Eight* ★

A Porn Star Kid's Cautionary Tale

I hated my mother. I hated her so much that I tried to sabotage everything she did, including her so-called porn ministry.

It all started when I was born.

Darker and hairier than my blonde porn star mom, I felt awkward and ugly. People noticed my "mixed" look and kids made fun of me.

"Werewolf!" they yelled and howled at me. I just punched them back in the face. I was a half-Asian little Karate kid who didn't take crap from anyone.

I was also *very* angry. I hated my mother and especially those stupid men she brought home. All the drunken men she dated would tell me they wanted to be my Daddy and I would start to feel so happy inside and think, *Wow, I get to be a part of a real family!*

But then they would leave again. And also, they touched me down there. I hated when they did that. It made me want to touch myself down there, too.

That's when I started masturbating at four years old. It made me feel good and anyway, it made the pain go away, at least for a little while. I also pretended to be a boy and do "things" to my stuffed animals. One time I found my mom's strapped on dildo and acted out sex with my teddy bear. It was weird how I knew how to use it. I probably learned it from my mother when I accidentally saw her porn movie.

She was wearing red. I was five years old.

At first I thought my Mom was a movie star but then I saw an old man pull out his "you know what" and stick it inside of her. I felt so dirty and gross. I thought she was a bad mommy and I hated her.

Then I masturbated. After a few minutes, I hated my life and wanted to die.

A voice helped me and said to me, "It's okay, Tiffany."

When I was finished the voice told me, "You should just kill yourself."

One day I found a knife in the middle of nowhere and I cut myself as hard as I could. I thought it would kill me but it didn't.

"It's okay," the voice said. "You can try again later when Mommy isn't looking."

I was desperately afraid of my mother. I knew she would slap me in the face and yell at me if I didn't do what she said. Sometimes when she wasn't looking, I tried her wigs on. I wanted to be just like her. I actually wanted to be *with* her. But she never had time for me.

I was invisible.

When the stupid men came over our house, my Mom gave me a beeper and told me to stay outside until she beeped me. I knew better than to come back in early or she would get mad and yell at me.

When I went outside to play, nobody noticed me.

When I was hungry, I went to the neighbor's house or my mom would buy me Chili fries at Wienerschnitzel's. Or sometimes I would go downstairs to get food and see a man with a video camera and my mom naked with another woman.

I got really scared and ran back upstairs.

When we lived in an old house with a bunch of people, I wanted attention so I crawled on my mom's friend's lap and asked him to have sex with me. He gave me a funny look.

One time my mom showed me love and gave me a chocolate Sundae. I was so happy but then I saw her pour her "drink" into my ice cream and I got really scared. The bottle had a black and white label. My Mommy made me eat it and then I passed out.

Whenever I tried to hug my mommy, I could tell she didn't want to touch me. I knew she didn't want me because I was ugly and half-Asian. She always told me I was nothing like her; that I was just a thing that appeared out of nowhere.

Kids told me I was a bastard. I was also sexually abused.

One night I spent the night with my mom's boyfriend and he told me to be quiet or I would have to sleep in bed with him naked. But when I laughed because he said the word "naked", he made me get into the bed with him. Then he made me touch his thing. Then he touched me down there. Everything got really confusing and became black.

I really hated my life. I dreaded waking up in the morning. To get through each day, I pretended I was in a movie and that whenever I woke up, it was a new movie. I became a great actress like my mother.

Then one day I met *another* one of my mom's boyfriends. He was tall and nicer than the others. He said he loved my Mommy but I didn't believe him. My five year old broken heart was already hardened by then.

The only thing I looked forward to was watching MTV. The music soothed me and took me to a place far away from my horrible life. At five years old, my favorite bands were Van Halen, Metallica, and Alice in Chains. I felt really close to the lead singer of Alice in Chains because he seemed really emotional.

I felt like that, too, I imagined.

Later on I heard that my favorite singer took his own life and that it took two weeks for people to finally notice. That's how I felt. Nobody would even notice if I was gone.

One day out of the blue my Mom married the nicer man and suddenly my new Dad's family was giving me gifts. They were really nice to me. But I still didn't trust them.

When I acknowledged my so-called Dad and called him, "Gary", he told me to call him Daddy instead.

"Okay, Gary," I simply replied and walked upstairs. No man could tell me anything.

As I grew older I began to cut myself. I felt ugly, disgusting and like a big loser because I masturbated. I thought I was the only one in the world who did that. I also felt really fat because I gained a lot of weight from emotional eating. Eating soothed me, especially chocolate.

In my junior high and high school years, I couldn't get along with anyone. Being a percussionist in the High School Band was the ONLY thing that made me get up in the morning. By then, I hated my life and felt like the biggest piece of shit in the world. I was big and brown and my flesh was fat and squishy. I felt like a literal piece of shit.

I turned into a rebel when my mother came out publicly with her story. I acted like I was okay with it, but deep inside I felt like she was trying to hurt me on purpose. I blamed God, too. How could He and my mother hurt me all over again, especially when our family finally had some peace?

I grew resentful and was full of rage. I began to self-mutilate myself even more. My mom always asked me why I wore long sleeves. She never knew it was because I cut myself. I also wore jeans to hide my scars and fat. In Washington I could get away with that but in California, my mom began to suspect something was wrong with me.

Finally, out of revenge and encouragement from evil voices, I tried to commit suicide on May 15, 2006, three days before my mother's birthday and ten days after she appeared on the 700 Club. I had just started taking Lexapro, an anti-depressant for severe PMS. At least that's what the doctors diagnosed me with. Little did anyone know I still struggled from the severe effects of child sexual abuse. All of those years my mother spent in deep recovery, I never healed.

Everyone just assumed I was healed.

When I found out at school I was failing my geometry class; that was the final icing on the cake. I wanted to prove myself so bad to my parents. I wanted to show people I wasn't a failure. In truth, I couldn't even read as a little girl. I got held back in Kindergarten and attended over thirteen schools due to the military moving our family around so much. I never received a solid chance to learn.

I felt like the world's biggest failure.

My relationships with friends were failing. My family was going through "porn" hell and lost the support of extended family. Now, I was failing at school. The same old voice came to me and said, "It's okay, Tiffany, just kill yourself and the pain will be over."

245

So I skipped my last class and drove home in my truck while laughing like an insane person. Suddenly the thought of me killing myself became the best idea in the world, kind of like the invention of electricity.

But God really had my mom reach out to me that day. Suddenly she called and said she wanted to spend some time with me at the nail salon. I told her I was busy but then my mom kept calling and said she felt like something was wrong and that she really needed to be with me.

"I don't want to go to the nail salon. I'm fine." I lied to her. But she knew something was wrong.

When I got home and out of the truck, I noticed our whole house looked like it had a black fog over it. I could literally hear Satan laughing at me. I couldn't fight him anymore. I felt high like I was on drugs. I looked around and noticed that every house looked beautiful but that our house looked black and disgusting.

I walked in and dropped everything by the door and went straight to the kitchen to find a knife. I didn't think twice about it and I started sawing away at my wrist like a violinist. I was crying violently and ferociously, totally out of control. I utterly hated my life and I slashed my wrist as deep as I could.

And then my mother called me. She said she sensed there was something very wrong with me and really wanted to talk to me. I hung up the phone and went to the bathroom where I passed out several times on the floor because of all the blood loss.

Suddenly I came back to reality and a powerful Voice said, "Get up." I looked around and didn't recognize what had happened. I started freaking out and God's Voice said to me to, "Calm down, Tiffany. I am here."

"What did I do, God? What did I do?" I cried out to God.

God calmly answered, "You cut your wrist. Don't worry. I need you to type in "Lexapro" in Google."

I immediately went to the computer and typed in Lexapro and read a warning about teenagers who killed themselves while taking the anti-depressant. God reassured me at that moment that I was not insane. I really felt His love and care for me in that moment.

When my mother came home and realized what had happened, her and my Dad immediately took me to the Emergency Room where the nurse asked me if I wanted to kill myself. I replied yes. Then she typed in the word suicide.

I looked over at my Dad and his head was lowered with tears streaming down his face. It was the worst moment of my life.

My parents were heartbroken. My poor mother was totally confused. She was sure God had told her to go public with her story and to start a ministry to help people in the porn industry and fight pornography and yet, her family was falling apart. That's when my mother started having serious health problems.

But she never gave up on me and in fact, she fought harder for me. She would come into my room and teach me God's Word and encourage me with Bible stories like the one about David in Ziklag. She taught me how to encourage myself in the Lord and to never *ever* give up. She told me how beautiful I was and shared Scriptures about God's incredible love for me. She didn't totally understand what I was going through, but she knew God's Word could heal me. She was living proof of that.

One day I couldn't stand the pain anymore and I told God either He needed to prove He was real or I was definitely going to kill myself. I threw the Bible up in the air and it landed on my bed and opened to Psalm 103:

Praise the LORD, O my soul, and forget not all his benefits, who forgives all your sins and heals all your diseases, who redeems your life from the pit and crowns you with love and compassion.

That is the day I really got saved.

As I began to stand on God's Word and heal the next few years, God sent me a humble and merciful man named Shane who became the love and joy of my life. I married the first boy I ever kissed on August 15, 2009, when I was twenty years old. I was *finally* given a real chance to heal and study God's Word without any interruption. Married to Shane and in his protection, God began to teach me about His great love for me. It's as if being married demonstrated the "oneness" and "specialness" God wanted to have with me. My parents had shown me a great example of love in a Christian marriage and now it was my turn to experience a loving relationship.

After a very long and difficult journey, I'm now back by my mother's side and ready to fight the good fight. I know it's an urgent fight, especially since God has utterly prepared me from the depths of hell. But I'm ready. I'm ready to take Satan on and destroy the works of darkness.

I don't masturbate anymore and I'm not angry anymore. If anything, I am filled with genuine compassion to help those who are hurting like I was. I am also filled with a holy fire for God's Truth and Justice to be spread throughout the earth. For such a time as this, I know I have been born and chosen by God to be His messenger.

My name is proof of that. My mother didn't know it at the time, but she named me "Tiffany" which means, "appearance of God".

Born of a prostitute, what are the odds?

But God had a perfect plan for my life and He has one for yours, too! Won't you let me pray for you today? Please say this prayer with me and meet the God "who heals all of your diseases, who redeems your life from the pit and crowns you with love and compassion."

Dear Father,
I want to know You. I believe that You sent Your Son Jesus
into the world to die for my sins and to heal all of my diseases
and to rescue me from the pit of hell and destruction. I ask you
to save me and cleanse me and to teach me Your ways and to
crown me with love and compassion. Thank you, Father, for
Your amazing love.
Amen

Our family loves you and is praying for you!

XXIX

★ *Admit One* ★

★ JOURNEY INTO HELL ★

★ *Chapter Twenty Nine* ★

The power of a prayer took on new meaning for my family. With my theology falling apart, our relatives upset with us, verbal attacks from the porn industry, rebukes from so-called Christians and other ministries trying to pull me into the Christian gossip game, I knew it was time to fall on my knees and pray until a I burned a hole into my shaggy brown carpet.

I was definitely *not* ready for an international porn ministry. I mean, how was I supposed to find spiritual mentors for THAT? But God assured me when I got down on my knees, that He would answer my desperate prayers and do *exceedingly* above all I could ask or think. I suddenly remembered a preacher's powerful words when he said, "No great move of God ever happens without great prayer."

I began to pray for specific things that I knew I needed in order to continue in the radical ministry God had called me to. Inspired by Billy Graham's autobiography, "Just as I Am", one thing I prayed for was for dedicated lifelong friends to come alongside of us, just like Billy had. At that time it was only my family up against a mounting porn war and we were already worn out.

Especially me.

From staph infections to severe anemia caused by hemorrhaging during my periods, I had barely started and I was already feeling sick. I remembered my spiritual mentor Pat's vital words when she warned me I would need to take better care of my health if I wanted to be a missionary. Experienced in world mission's outreach, she warned me. But I didn't listen. I was so built up in the "Champion" spiritual ways, I didn't think much about the "physical" aspect of ministry. In fact, God also warned me about my health. When I first started the ministry in 2004 I weighed a whopping 198 pounds and God warned me to lose weight to get in shape for the powerful mission ahead.

I truly did not understand the vast imminent ministry God called me to. In my mind, I was a Christian mom and Bible teacher who lived in Bakersfield and fought a little porn on the side. Still really involved with my children's school and my Theology classes, I barely noticed when my interviews appeared on the news or the radio. Okay, maybe I noticed a little. Sure, it was exciting *at first* to see myself on television or hear myself on the radio but seriously, I became so busy doing the actual work of the ministry that I didn't watch or listen to half of the interviews I did. In 2006, I was up to about 1-2 radio shows a week tearing the lid off of pornography -- and that's when all the porn stars, prostitutes and strippers started contacting me.

Truly, that's when the *real* ministry began.

Hours and hours of non-stop mental illness and pornographic complaints coming through my telephone into my already stressed out Christian ears. I listened to *hundreds* of women tell me their problems all the way from Germany! Obscene things I had never even heard of entered into my reformed mind and although I became confused about the "pornographic" nature of my ministry, I still kept going. The compassion of the Lord Jesus filled my heart for the wrecked women who cried out for help from all over the world.

Suddenly I found myself immersed in MySpace for hours talking to porn stars, strippers, prostitutes, phone sex girls, wives, husbands, youth and everyone else under the sun who cried out for help from pornography and the sex industry. I had developed such a deep love and passion to see *all* people be healed that I totally forgot about my own health!

But the call of God continued to grow and next thing you know, I started sniffing out porn conventions in January of 2006. My pastor of the church we were semi-attending offered to rent a room to reach out to porn stars. I was overjoyed! Then two weeks before the outreach, the pastor changed his mind and said we were reaching out to porn addicts instead. I was bummed. I also wondered how he planned on getting porn addicts to leave a porn convention and receive help for porn addiction.

But we all put our trust in God and a small team from Bakersfield headed for Las Vegas to the Adult Entertainment Expo 2006. Well, at least we headed for a rented room close by to the expo. We split up in teams and I ended up being one of the few that went inside the actual convention. Unfamiliar with the modern day porn industry, a whole new pornographic world opened up to me as I stood there in horror staring at violent images in front of me.

Video after video of women's faces being ripped back while grotesque men violently penetrated them from behind became too much for me. To my great disgust, I turned my head to witness the hundreds to thousands of male fans standing around me watching the violent videos with extreme delight. I couldn't believe my Christian eyes! I had never seen so many desperate demonized men in one place. Starving ravenous wolves staring at the porn stars as if it was their last meal, I wanted the hell out of there. But the Lord told me to get out the anointing oil instead and lay hands on all the booths. Obedient to His Voice, I began to pray through the power of Holy Spirit, and suddenly a matter of life and death became clear to me. The urgency I felt was unexplainable as I went from booth to booth casting out demons under my breath in the name of Jesus Christ. The powerful warrior in me rose up and I knew I was battling for the eternal destiny of souls.

It was a day of reckoning. It was also a Day of the Lord's Favor.

Suddenly, women *and* men started leaving porn. I hadn't even ministered personally to some of them but God *Himself* was rescuing them. It was amazing to watch the hand of God move so powerfully in the midst of so much evil. I found it even more amazing that the very ones I prayed for at the booths in the convention, some of them were the same ones now getting out!

Truly, the power of prayer took on an even newer meaning in my life. Inspired by God's amazing rescue of women in porn, I became a powerful praying woman.

As I continued to minister to women in the sex industry, I learned that God was *already* on the move and had rescued thousands of women out of the entire sex industry, including strippers, prostitutes, phone sex operators and more. Amazingly, a world-wide movement of God had already begun but in

2006, things began to move quickly, especially when I saw a host of sex industry ministries popping up all over the web.

I had never seen anything like it. I hadn't even read about anything that could describe what God was doing in the earth. Surely, God was up to something HUGE! And here's the big kicker, I was chosen to be one of His leaders in the sex industry emancipation movement!

Holy Jehosaphat! "Who am I?" I kept asking God.

"Just stay humble, Shelley. You're going to need some serious humility for this," God along with the rest of the Christian world emphatically warned me and so I bought a book on the greatness of humility. I knew, honestly, I was not humble enough for an outreach of this caliber. I wasn't near ready to be a "Mother Teresa" to the porn industry. No way. I was a wretch and enjoyed the interviews and camera *way* too much in the beginning.

But God was faithful to work out a cure for my enjoyment of any part of the new public ministry he called me to. To begin my school of humility, He lovingly sent me other porn ministries to drive me crazy. Our immature fights along with my deteriorating health and mix in some satanic warfare and hours of listening to mentally ill and sexually abused women, oh yeah, I was definitely being humbled.

Heck, I needed it. I was such an idiot in the beginning.

But I digress.

Wait, let me regress. I am still an idiot.

Okay, now I truly digress.

Seriously though, God knew I needed more humility for the sudden public interest in the hardcore testimony of Ex Porn Star Shelley Lubben in 2006. What I consider my "break out" year into the public, I started receiving speaking invitations throughout the United States and media requests to appear on major television networks for both Christian and secular television shows.

Finally, I thought. *I'm doing what I was created for!*

My first major Christian television appearance was on the 700 Club. Filmed at my home in Bakersfield, I also appeared LIVE on the show on May 5, 2006. Filled with the Spirit of God and the saving testimony of Jesus Christ, 700 Club producers reported that 546 people got saved during the hour I appeared on the show.

I was preaching the hardcore Gospel of Jesus Christ now!

And of course, there was satanic backlash. Satan wasn't going to let an ex porn star get away with a testimony like that in front of an audience of porn struggling Christians! Hell no, he made sure that TEN DAYS LATER he powerfully orchestrated for my 17 year old daughter to try and commit suicide by slicing her wrist with a huge jagged knife.

If you only *knew* the pain our family experienced.

I was sure it was time to quit but God totally disagreed with me. In fact, He made me preach the day after the attack on my daughter at a Celebrate Recovery meeting. Imagine the slap to Satan's punk face. A message preached out of pure suffering, I saw God powerfully touch and heal every person at that meeting. Oh yeah, God rocked it!

Filled with bewilderment over the new warfare my family was in, we skipped the opportunity to reach out to porn stars at the 2007 Adult Entertainment Expo in January. God made it clear I was *not* to go and to stay really close to Him and *learn.* Anyway, the porn ministries were fighting and it became way too much for me to partake in anymore so God warned me to separate myself.

It wasn't easy to separate because I had been taught so much about teamwork and unity at the Champion's Centre. But at the same time I could *not* stomach the gimmicky and overly grace-packed message being offered to thousands of pornified people whose lives were a living and future hell. They needed the pure unadulterated Gospel of Jesus Christ, not some 30 foot erect Wally the Wiener blowup penis I saw "popped up" at one porn ministry's booth. I understood they were trying to be relevant, but seriously, they did not know the power of God's Word. Especially, when I also discovered a video on their web site about how God kills kittens every time someone masturbates. The blatant irreverence towards God's holy attributes, I was horrified. No, I *knew* better than to stay very involved with them. But of course, for the sake of the babes coming to several of our porn ministries to receive help at the same time, I *tried* to bite my tongue and use more wisdom in my dealings with other ministries and organizations.

Just like porn, I quietly backed away from the elite porn ministry circle and followed God into No-Man's Land.

That's when the question of the century burned inside of my mind: How could I reach out to the porn stars and pornographers and porn fans in love at a porn convention and yet not compromise God's Truth?

While I pondered that question and continued my online outreach to porn stars and porn addicts, I somehow ended up preaching the Gospel and my testimony to an audience of 2,000 Christian men in Bend, Oregon.

Incredibly nervous but filled with the Holy Spirit, I boldly called upon men in the audience who were struggling with a pornography addiction to stand up and receive healing through the power of Jesus Christ. At first only about 30% of the men stood up but then God told me to call more out on the carpet and so I did.

"God said there's MORE of you and to stand up! Whoever stands up will be delivered today!" I shouted out into the dark arena.

Almost immediately another 40% of the men stood up. It was an amazing view from the big stage and suddenly it matched the exact vision Jesus gave me when I was six years old.

Filled with extreme emotions, I tried to fight back the tears while I humbly praised God for all He was doing through me and around me. I couldn't believe it. I honestly *still* don't believe it.

God proved faithful over and over and fruit from my ministry began to pop up everywhere. Messages of gratitude were sent from people all over the world for my courage to tell my story and boldly declare the Gospel. God's goodness toward me and my family overwhelmed me.

By the end of 2007 and a victorious online outreach to porn stars and porn addicts, regular appearances on both secular and Christian TV networks and traveling and speaking to churches and organizations sharing the truth about pornography and the Gospel, God began to move in our hearts for an even greater move to heal the world from pornography.

Due to the outcry of millions of hurting people and the need for someone to go into the porn industry with firsthand knowledge and a heart to rescue, my husband and I went to a lawyer to officially start up the Pink Cross Foundation: the faith based non-profit organization that would be the first to financially and emotionally assist women and men out of the porn industry. No longer would we only meet with the porn stars privately or online, it was time to boldly step into their world and reach out to them in a tangible way and share the truth and love of Jesus Christ.

At first I had no clue how that looked but fortunately, I had taken the time to build relationships with many of the people in porn. I genuinely loved these people. I loved them so much that I worried if my outreach may hurt or embarrass them in a major way so I cried out to God for more wisdom.

But God assured me over time that there was little I could do to embarrass people who were used to publicly exposing their sexually diseased bodies. These people just needed hardcore love and a shot of reality and I was the one to give it to them.

So, I went for it and called up the porn show management to reserve a booth for the Erotica LA 2008 convention. Then I hurried to try and raise money for the Goliath-sized outreach. I spent months trying to convince people to support the powerful move of God in the porn industry.

As our team of ex porn stars and recovering porn addicts prepared to minister in one of the most hostile environments known to Christianity, God also prepared the hearts of California lawmakers to hear a firsthand account from someone who had lived to tell about the secondary negative effects of pornography.

Lord, have mercy.

Contacted in January of 2008 by the office of Assemblymember Charles M. Calderon, he wanted me to help him push the Porn Tax bill that would tax the porn industry a whopping 25%. This would bring some serious cash into poverty-stricken California as well as help ameliorate the secondary negative effects of pornography.

Suddenly, I was knee deep in a political world that I wasn't ready for. At least, I didn't think so but God proved me wrong and used my testimony along with Daphne, my compadre and former adult entertainer, to expose the ENTIRE California adult industry. Now God was going after the whole adult world, not just the porn industry.

Lord have mercy, again!

On May 12, 2008, my family, Daphne and I walked into the California State Capitol building and it immediately felt like home. I never felt so sure of anything in my life. Energized by the powerful people and decision making going on around me, I fell in *love* with the super power system and dreamed of one day becoming a public servant. Thoughts of reforming California danced in my overwhelmed stressed out head.

I have to admit, as much as I loved it though, I felt really nervous. When Assemblymember Calderon announced there were too many people on the opposing side of the bill and we had to move to a larger building, that's when reality smacked me hard in the face.

Oh crap, I'm about to testify against the multi-billion dollar porn industry, I thought. *How the heck did I get so far in such a short time?* I inquired of God.

As usual, He smiled back and said His two famous words, "Trust Me."

Though the bill never passed ultimately, in August 2008, the bill did pass out of the Assembly Revenue and Taxation Committee and it was a huge victory. Suddenly California began to understand the horrible porn problem as well as public service agencies wanted to get behind me. Of course they did. They hoped I would save their jobs!

But imagine what it was like for me to go to the Erotica LA convention only two weeks later after I first testified against the porn industry in the state legislature.

Not pretty.

The satanic backlash worsened and I was in the doctor's office almost every week for my own secondary negative effects from pornography. Back on my knees, I prayed to God for serious strategies from heaven to continue the fight against pornography and still remain in one piece!

As I prayed, I remembered the humble words of Jesus in Matthew 5:

Blessed are the meek, for they will inherit the earth.

Meekness means controlled strength. Holy Spirit also taught me that humility would be my number one weapon in the fight against pornography. He was right.

Obviously I can't share all of the heavenly strategies that I've been given but...

Eyebrows lifted.

Let's just say I pursued humility, walked in love as best I could, began to pray all day and night to the True Most High God, asked other dedicated people to pray and of course, I worked *really* hard. I also learned to rely solely on God's Spirit, especially when I was utterly beside myself with *no one* to understand the hell I was going through.

When no one had the high wisdom or advice to help me continue to pioneer the "ministry turned mission" God called me to, only God's Spirit could speak to me. 1 John 2:27 became the hardcore reality of my life:

As for you, the anointing you received from him remains in you, and you do not need anyone to teach you. But as his anointing teaches you about all things and as that anointing is real, not counterfeit— just as it has taught you, remain in him.

I finally understood what that Scripture meant and began to learn how to totally trust the leading of the Holy Spirit. That was one of the most difficult things to do, especially with so many voices telling me otherwise!

My parents told me one thing. My mentors warned me with another. Christians, Muslims, Catholics, Mormons, Atheists and everybody else told me their views. They all wanted to give their opinion about my porn mission and which god to follow but my God warned me and said, "Follow Me."

It became extremely difficult when even my own husband expressed doubts about the mission that God gave us. Suddenly, another question burned in our minds: Were we really called by God to lead an international anti-pornography outreach mission and allow our family to fall apart because of it?

According to the Google search I did on "ministry burnout", our family should have hung up their combat boots a long time ago.

But God made it crystal clear to me that I was not to look to the right or to the left and that I was to continue to follow the anointing. Wherever His power was, that was where I was sup-posed to go. And if there wasn't any tangible power, to get down on my feeble knees and cry out for more strength and humility.

I also realized during this extreme learning time that I was being crucified and entirely emptied of myself due to the fleshly arrogance that still dwelt within me. Front row in the school of humility, I became desperate and read only books written by Saints who had already been there and done that.

Mother Teresa, St. John of the Cross, St. Francis of Assisi, St. Teresa of Avila, St. Paul and the list goes on. Unable to receive any relief from the contemporary grace-filled prosperity Gospel teachers, I turned to historical Saints of God for help.

It all began when I started having horrific nightmares for the first time in seven years. Images of women and children being brutally raped entered my mind as well as terrorizing dreams of me in great battle against Satan and super-sized demons. Truly, I thought I left my body every night to fight vicious inhuman entities in another world. Suddenly my bedroom became a war zone and my husband and I grew very perplexed.

It got so bad, I couldn't even have enjoyable sex anymore because of me being re-traumatized by the continual porno-graphic images and information I was daily exposed to. My condition became so terrible that I actually had to replace my shredded bed sheets because of the holes I tore through them. Think about it. A woman and mother leading a porn fight and a porn outreach to porn stars while trying to help thousands of people recover from porn addiction while *also* spending endless hours researching the porn industry in order to win a porn fight while in constant communication with other porn advocates and ministries. Oh yeah, you better believe I was hurting from porn.

But you know what hurt the most? The fact that whenever I put a much needed prayer request up on the Internet, I typically received cruel rebukes or thoughtless suggestions from the greater part of responses. Only a few of my truest and most thoughtful friends understood to keep the advice to a minimum and instead to turn the heat up on the prayers.

That's when I realized the condition of the Church was even *worse* than I had previously imagined. When I desperately needed prayer and encouragement to continue an excruciating fight against porn, I largely received compassionless and faithless suggestions from so-called people of God.

My heart was utterly broken. I never felt so alone in my life. Even the old porn days weren't as bad as what I was going through in 2008.

My heart was even more shattered when I reached out to certain organizations for prayer *and* much needed assistance, including churches in the San Fernando Valley area where the porn industry is located and guess what? They wouldn't even give me business cards to pass out to porn stars to invite them to church.

What the hell was their church doing in Porn Valley? I angrily questioned.

All I wanted was some prayer and church business cards to pass out to the porn stars. I even volunteered to drive down to the area and "escort" porn stars into the big beautiful church on Sherman Way but they said they needed to talk to their Board of Directors first.

I was livid to say the least. And then of course, I got a taste of commercial Christianity. I swore if I ever had a chance to get on a certain Christian television stage, I would rip up the gaudy gold chairs and cast them straight into the pit of hell for ignoring the pandemic porn problem in the earth. But then it got even worse. I discovered from emails I received from Pastors, Bishops, Missionaries and Priests around the world, that the Church of Jesus Christ, no matter what affiliation or denomination, is the *main* contributor to the destructive porn industry!

AHHHHH!!! I screamed at the top of my lungs in my back yard while spewing to God about my utter disgust with these people who supposedly belonged to Him. Here I was giving my life's blood for God's enormous move in the earth, and the vast majority of His people were masturbating to porn.

Holy Shit!

I wasn't the same anymore and the recovered Champion Mom and woman named Shelley disappeared and someone else resurrected in my body. That's when I went out and bought an eight foot wooden staff at Home Depot and began to pray and aim it in the air towards major government super powers and Christian organizations.

It was a time of reckoning between God and His people and the earth dwellers.

Yeah, I was starting to be in a very bad prophetic mood by the end of 2008. Not great for outreach but definitely perfect for a vicious porn fight. God knew what He was doing and sure enough, I boldly showed up at the legislature again and testified to the extreme horrors of the illegally operating and hazardous porn industry.

And you know what; the State of California started to listen! Especially when God instructed me to bring a powerful pack of recovering porn stars He freshly saved out of the industry to *also* testify about the horrible work conditions in the porn industry. Truly, God in His infinite wisdom had created a small army of "ardent" women to take down one of the greatest evils in all of history.

Both Martin Luthers stand up in heaven and applaud the ex porn stars!

But there was a price to pay for that kind of victory and history making and certainly, my family and other Pink Cross team members paid it. With daily satanic attacks on our lives and even physical threats by the opposition, we cried out to God for hardcore reinforcement.

The next thing you know a group of Southern California law enforcement Chaplains wanted to join our cause and even ordain us for the mission!

Only God could have come up with that one.

On April 4, 2009, Garrett and I became officially ordained as Chaplains of the Order of Saint Martin, in the tradition of Martin of Tours. Suddenly, our anti-porn mission began to look like a real Reformation as God deliberately threw "Martin" hints at us. I knew right then what I was called to do.

To whoever much is given, of him will much be required.

That would be me, I recited Luke 12:48 in my head as I looked up into heaven at the "rest" of the reformers nodding their heads in agreement. I knew too much and God Almighty expected a lot from me.

God announced to me I was an official Reformer in 2008 and on my way to becoming a mortified Saint.

Yes, I almost died several times because of this ministry. Okay, so this book is about truth, right? So, I'm going to tell you the truth behind Shelley Lubben and her wrecked family. We literally gave up our beautiful perfect life and everything we ever cared about or held dear to our hearts in order to help YOU who continue to view pornography and ignore the impenitent porn problem.

Holy Spirit enters to speak but patiently waits for Shelley to finish her story.

With our family almost completely wrecked by the end of 2008, only our truest friends saw us through our darkest hours. I admit, I had my "Elijah" moments and thought I was the only prophet in town who cared *passionately* about the problem of porn, but through the years God revealed to me thousands of loving and committed people who don't and won't give up!

One of those beautiful people is Dr. Judith Reisman, world renowned pornography expert, powerful author and Jewish woman who is in *my* opinion, the *greatest* of unsung heroes in our nation. She naturally took the time to mentor me, encourage me excessively, taught me about our nation's history and how the greatest generation of our time was sabotaged by a porno- graphic assault by a man named Kinsey. My heart broke and bled as she explained the vast devastation that Playboy and other pornography pioneers also caused our nation. Our na- tion's greatest men had been completely destroyed by pornography.

Sent by God to rejuvenate me with powerful ammunition to help me continue the fight against pornography and see God set His people free from its devastation, I realized that God put a Jew and a Christian together to do His powerful work in the earth.

It was prophetic and supernatural!

At the same time Dr. Reisman began to mentor me about the pornographic assault on our nation, fraudulent sex scientists and how they experimented on young children to gather infor- mation on orgasms, as well as handing me over thirty years of her experience literally on a silver platter, I was *also* knee deep in the trenches with Pink Cross Foundation in a year of non- stop outreaches at porn conventions.

My team was on fire and doing the impossible. We boldly walked into porn conventions with an eight foot wide banner that declared, "Porn Is Not Glamorous" and erected it above our pink and black booth. Causing everyone who walked by to take notice, our team offered education, prayer, hardcore truth and huge amounts of love to thousands of porn stars and porn fans. By then I had been emptied of most of my humanity and was so full of God's Spirit that I also put up the Latin Inscription of the Cross above our banner. *I was on a mission* to tear down the high places of idolatry and establish the Kingdom of God.

Filled with a superior measure of the Holy Spirit, my newly ordained team marched around with Bibles in hand and aimed them at the major porn companies praying down the judgment of God. God also instructed us to march around the Hustler booth seven times and to shout out when we were done. We also went to every booth and aimed our prayers directly at porn stars and declared chains to be broken off of them and to be completely set free. It was time for the porn industry to officially come down. It was time for God's creations to be declared free to live and do something powerful and amazing with their lives. NO longer would God tolerate the pornographic slave trade of human beings. It was TIME for thousands of men and women to be set free from the porn industry and at the same time, God was formulating a powerful plan to heal His Church.

After our last major convention outreach in Las Vegas, in January 2010, I had become ridiculously confident in God's ability to go above and beyond like He originally promised me. With a powerful team by my side, thousands of wonderful people around the world praying by now and the loving support of true friends, I realized there was absolutely nothing impossible for God. My life was living proof of that over and over. From drugged out prostitute and porn star to Betty Crocker cupcake Mom to international Reformer and Champion of the Faith, only God could have orchestrated anything like that!!

And that's not all.

God topped Himself and proved to me through the name of the street I live on what the nature of my True call is. I didn't realize it at the time we bought our house in Bakersfield, but God supernaturally orchestrated for us to live on Elias Avenue. Yes, Elias is Greek for Elijah, the name of the fieriest prophet in the Old Testament who took on 850 false prophets of Baal and called down the Fire of God on them. That's right; the 850 prophets could not triumph over ONE prophet who knew God.

I'll let you think about that one for a minute.

★ CIRCUS MAXIMUS PROPHECY ★

It began with the rape of the Sabine women.

The imperial Roman Emperor held chariot races that were so distracting, that "nobody had eyes or thoughts for anything else." While the Sabine men enjoyed the races, their unmarried women were abducted by the Romans to become their wives.

But for the next thousand years, chariot races distracted Rome.

Meeting the demands of the Roman citizenry for mass public entertainment, chariot racing became the most viewed event at the world's largest and first circus: Circus Maximus.

It was spectacular.

The greatest Roman entertainment complex of all time, over 200,000 spectators indulged in gambling, shows, prostitution, and pleasure. Admission was free to "the greatest show on earth" and anyone could attend, even the poor of Rome.

The rape twisted entertainment attracted Romans from every corner.

Highly-charged fans, sectioned off into "factions" of Reds, Greens, Blues and Whites, cheered the almost naked Charioteers. Drawn from the dregs of society, the slave horse drivers affiliated with teams were supported by large businesses that invested heavily in the training and upkeep of the hot-blooded thoroughbreds. The colorful team jerseys provided drivers with names, and fans would often hurl violent enthusiasms, as well as aim curse amulets punctured with nails, at the Reds, Greens, Blues and Whites.

It was a cursed occasion.

Under the spirit of what the Romans called *furor circensis*, the name for the mass hysteria the races induced, fans ate and drank to excess, and fights were common among the pounding bleachers.

Excitement, risk and frenzy were vital ingredients for a champion race.

After seven savage laps, which would include as many as 12 chariots at any one time, the drivers who managed not to be upended or killed and finish in the top three took home prizes. They became deified super-stars, like Scorpus who won 2,000 races before dying in splendor at 27. They were also made extraordinarily wealthy.

Drivers who didn't survive were thrown from their broken or overturned chariots and trampled and killed by the charging horses, or dragged to their early deaths.

Erected high atop platforms, the emperors loved to watch the bloodthirsty games.

From sunrise to sunset, one quarter of Rome's population came to witness a deathly average of 25 races per day. During breaks from the races, the Circus also held a variety of religious ceremonies, wild-beast hunting, mock battles and even the unexpected gladiator exhibition found its way into the circus. The majority of Christian martyrdom in the sprawling capital city also took place at the Roman Circus Maximus.

In 64 A.D. the Roman Emperor Caesar Nero attempted to systematically exterminate all people who professed faith in the newfound Christian religion. Under his evil rule, Romans witnessed the worst atrocities upon his victims; he did not just kill Christians, he made them suffer extremely. Nero enjoyed dipping the Christians in tar, and impaling them on poles around his palace, he would then light them on fire, and yell: "Now you truly are the light of the world."

Nero also performed many other kinds of torture, often killing them in the grand Circus Maximus in front of large crowds of spectators where he perpetrated some of his most gruesome murders. Here he would wrap Christians up in animal skins and throw them to lions, or dogs that would viciously tear these men and women apart in front of thousands of "entertained" spectators. At other times he would crucify them, and after the crowd would get bored, he would set the Christians on fire.

The whole of Rome was in an uproar as they witnessed Christians executed for public entertainment. It was a fantastic spectacle and not much different than today.

Take heed, Christians, the spirit of Nero is alive and well. While you strayed from Me and chose slave drivers in their bloodthirsty races and did not return to My love, I gave you over to your hysterical lust and now you belong to Nero. He has dipped you in the worldwide wax and impaled you around his pornographic palace. You are now officially the Light of the world.

Welcome to the abomination of desolation.

Listen to the prophet Isaiah.

Chapter 58:

"Shout it aloud, do not hold back.

Raise your voice like a trumpet.

Declare to my people their rebellion

and to the house of Jacob their sins.

For day after day they seek me out;

they seem eager to know my ways,

as if they were a nation that does what is right

and has not forsaken the commands of its God.

They ask me for just decisions

and seem eager for God to come near them.

'Why have we fasted,' they say, 'and you have not seen it?

Why have we humbled ourselves, and you have not noticed?'

"Yet on the day of your fasting, you do as you please

and exploit all your workers.

Your fasting ends in quarreling and strife,

and in striking each other with wicked fists.

You cannot fast as you do today

and expect your voice to be heard on high.

Is this the kind of fast I have chosen,

only a day for a man to humble himself?

Is it only for bowing one's head like a reed

and for lying on sackcloth and ashes?

Is that what you call a fast, a day acceptable to the LORD?

"Is not this the kind of fasting I have chosen:

to loose the chains of injustice

and untie the cords of the yoke,

to set the oppressed free

and break every yoke?

Is it not to share your food with the hungry

and to provide the poor wanderer with shelter—

when you see the naked, to clothe him,

and not to turn away from your own flesh and blood?

273

TRUTH BEHIND THE FANTASY OF PORN

Then your light will break forth like the dawn,

and your healing will quickly appear;

then your righteousness will go before you,

and the glory of the LORD will be your rear guard.

Then you will call, and the LORD will answer;

you will cry for help, and he will say: Here am I.

"If you do away with the yoke of oppression,

with the pointing finger and malicious talk,

and if you spend yourselves in behalf of the hungry

and satisfy the needs of the oppressed,

then your light will rise in the darkness,

and your night will become like the noonday.

The LORD will guide you always;

he will satisfy your needs in a sun-scorched land

and will strengthen your frame.

You will be like a well-watered garden,

like a spring whose waters never fail.

CIRCUS MAXIMUS PROPHECY

Your people will rebuild the ancient ruins

and will raise up the age-old foundations;

you will be called Repairer of Broken Walls,

Restorer of Streets with Dwellings.

"If you keep your feet from breaking the Sabbath

and from doing as you please on my holy day,

if you call the Sabbath a delight

and the LORD'S holy day honorable,

and if you honor it by not going your own way

and not doing as you please or speaking idle words,

then you will find your joy in the LORD,

and I will cause you to ride on the heights of the land

and to feast on the inheritance of your father Jacob."

The mouth of the LORD has spoken.

End Notes

I: Under the Big Top

1. Regan Starr Interview. Talk Magazine, http://www.cwfa.org/articles/ 3838/LEGAL/pornography/index.htm, February 2001.
2. Porn Star Jersey Jaxin Interview. http://www.shelleylubben.com /audio/ Jersey1.mp3
3. Becca Brat Interview. http://www.shelleylubben.com/porn-stars-speak-out-stds-drugs-and-abuse-0, May, 2006.
4. Christian XXX. "Christian Sings the Blues". January 2008. http:// cwians.typepad.com/christian_sings_the_blues/2008/01/index.html
5. Shelley Lubben. *AIDS, Suicide, Homicide and Drug Related Deaths since 1999.* http://www.shelleylubben.com/sites/default/files/PornFactoid 2009deaths_lubben.pdf
6. Michelle Avanti Interview. http://www.shelleylubben.com/shelleys-blog/shelleylubben/06/3/2009/michelle-avanti-leaves-porn
7. Jasyn Jones. *The Pornographication of American Culture.* April 23, 2003. The Daily Utah Chronicle web site. http://www.dailyutahchronicle .com/opinion/the-pornographication-of-american-culture-1.362967
8. Facts and TV Statistics. http://www.parentstv.org/ptc/facts/media facts.asp
9. Porn Star doctor Sharon Mitchell, "We keep the adult entertainment industry safe." Video at http://www.youtube.com/watch?v=5G1AIgh _X3E
10. Shelley Lubben. *Aids Related Deaths in the U.S. Porn Industry since 1985.* http://www.shelleylubben.com/sites/default/files/AIDS_related _deaths_lubben_0.pdf
11. Rong-Gong Lin II. *"Porn Star recalls nightmare of testing HIV positive."* http://articles.latimes.com/2009/jun/15/local/me-porn -hiv15
12. Porn Star doctor Sharon Mitchell, Founder of AIM (Adult Industry Medical Healthcare Foundation). *Porn Legend Sharon Mitchell - Interview With Court.* http://www.sharonmitchell.plazadiscounts.com/ page15.html
13. Johnathon E. Fielding, M.D., M.P.H. *Adult Film Industry Health Report.* http://www.shelleylubben.com/sites/default/files/LA_Public_Health_ 9-17-09.pdf

14. Kami Andrews. Interview with Luke Ford on September 15, 2004. http://www.lukeisback.com/stars/stars/kami_andrews. htm

15. New York Post web site. *"Marital stress in the X-treme."* http://www. nypost.com/p/pagesix/marital_stress_in_the_treme_qCVvNWMkSQ vDPkseFQh58M

II: Send in the Clowns

16. Based upon in-depth interviews and public testimonies by pornography employees, we estimate 90% are adult survivors of childhood sexual abuse. These data are considered reasonable based upon the extant data from established governmental statistical findings as follows: 1 in 4 girls is sexually abused before the age of 18. (http://www.cdc.gov/nccdphp/ace/prevalence.htm, ACE Study - Prevalence - Adverse Childhood Experiences); 1 in 6 boys is sexually abused before the age of 18. (http://www.cdc.gov/nccdphp/ace/ prevalence.htm, CE Study - Prevalence - Adverse Childhood Experiences); An estimated 39 million survivors of childhood sexual abuse exist in America today. (Abel, G., Becker, J., Mittelman , M., Cunningham-Rathner, J., Rouleau, J., & Murphy, W. 1987). Self reported sex crimes on non-incarcerated paraphiliacs. Journal of Interpersonal Violence, 2(1), 3-[25]

17. Dusk in Autumn Blog. *At what age are females at their hottest?* http:// akinokure.blogspot.com/2008/03/at-what-age-are-females-at-their. html, March 25, 2008.

18. April Garris. The Porn Effect Blog. "Myth 2 Exposed." http://www. whodoesithurt.com/april-garris/177-april-garris, March 8, 2010.

19. Adam Higginbotham. *The porn broker.* October 9, 2004, Telegraph Magazine, presented by The Age.

20. Shelley Lubben. *Aids, Suicide, Homicide and Drug Related Deaths since 1999.* http://www.shelleylubben.com/sites/default/files/PornFactoid 2009deaths_lubben.pdf

21. *Dead Porn Stars.* http://www.rame.net/faq/deadporn/

22. Glenn Peoples. *Analysis: Important Sales Trends You Need To Know.* http://www.billboard.biz/bbbiz/content_display/industry/e3i4ad94 ea6265fac02d4c813c0b6a93ca2, June 2, 2010.

23. Nominations for 2010 AVN Awards Announced. http://business. avn.com/articles/Nominations-for-2010-AVN-Awards-Announced-370904.html, December 2, 2009.

24. The Dead Rock Stars Club web site. http://thedeadrockstarsclub.com/ deadrock.html

25. The Recording Industry Association of America (RIAA). http://www.riaa.com/aboutus.php
26. Ibid., 20.
27. Kaiser Daily HIV/AIDS report. *Group Says HIV 'Outbreak' Contained Among Adult Film Actors; L.A. Health Officials Obtain Workers' Medical Record.* http://www.kaisernetwork.org/daily_reports/rep_index.cfm?DR_ID=23346, April 23, 2004.
28. Rev. Daniel R. Jennings. *The Average Life Expectancy Of A Porn Star.* http://danielrjennings.org/TheAverageLifeExpectancyOf APornStar

XXVII: To Hell with Paradise

29. Blazing Grace. *Statistics and Information on Pornography in the USA.* http://www.blazinggrace.org/cms/bg/pornstats

About the Author

Shelley Lynn Lubben, born on the heels of revolution on May 18, 1968, is one of the world's leading advocates in the anti-pornography movement. A former pornographic actress who performed under the stage name of Roxy, she left the sex industry in 1994 when she caught Genital Herpes, a non-curable disease.

Upon her eight year recovery at the Champion's Centre in Tacoma, Washington, she reentered society as a new Champion woman and began teaching and preaching in prisons and rescue missions in Central California. Ordained as a Chaplain with the Order of Saint Martin, Shelley is also a graduate of Vision International University where she received a Bachelor's degree in Theological Studies.

Now, fifteen years into recovery, Shelley has appeared on both Christian and secular television and radio shows and speaks out passionately about the harms of pornography as well as shares her inspirational story of redemption through Jesus Christ.

Shelley also serves as the Executive Director of Pink Cross Foundation, a nonprofit organization that offers hope, healing and support to adult industry workers around the world.

Shelley Lubben is sought worldwide to speak, educate, testify, and counsel individuals, organizations, professionals and governments regarding the illegally operating porn industry, pornography addiction, recovery from sexual abuse and the sex industry and the Champion life. Shelley is a mother of three beautiful daughters and married to Mr. Wonderful, Garrett Lubben, for fifteen years.

Resources

For more resources on the topics of pornography addiction, sexual abuse, the truth about porn and the Champion teachings, please visit Shelley's web site at *www.shelleylubben.com*

- ✓ Information and articles on the truth about pornography and how to recover from porn addiction.

- ✓ Information and articles on how to recover from sexual abuse and the sex industry.

- ✓ Stories from other ex porn stars and former adult entertainers to educate you thoroughly on the truth about the "adult" sex slave trade.

- ✓ Videos and audios of Shelley Lubben sharing her testimony.

- ✓ Help forums for those struggling with porn addiction and private forums for women recovering from the sex industry at *www.thepinkcross.org*

Learn more about Pink Cross Foundation, a faith-based IRS approved public charity dedicated to reaching out to adult industry workers offering emotional, financial and transitional support, at *www.thepinkcross.org*

To be continued…

Made in the USA
Charleston, SC
31 October 2010